Tai Chi
Fighting & Healing

Paul Brecher

GW00725844

Published in London by
JEDZAK BOOKS
PO BOX 13219
LONDON NW11 7WS
ENGLAND UK

A catalogue record for this title is
available from The British Library
ISBN 0-9542425-0-5

First Published 2002

Acknowledgment

Erle Montaigue is the Head of The World Taiji (Tai chi) Boxing Association, his martial and healing ability and willingness to communicate his knowledge make him a living treasure of the martial arts community. If it was not for his great efforts to preserve the art, then The Old Yang Style of Taiji (Tai chi) might never have been revealed to any one in the west.

This book contains an overview of the whole of the Old Yang Style Taiji (Tai chi) system, its forms, fight sequences and training methods and a detailed explanation of its many special aspects like qi gong (internal power), fa jin (explosive energy strikes) and dim mak (acupuncture point striking).

My students look to me for information and explanations about all these things and I in turn look to my teacher, Erle Montaigue. He is a direct link back to one of the greatest traditional martial arts of China and a shining light in the martial arts world who has illuminated many of the previously obscure and hidden aspects of the internal styles.

He has already produced many excellent training videos and written many books explaining in detail almost all the individual parts of the style. I thought that to complement this already excellent and informative encycrpedea of knowledge I would write a book that was an overview of the whole of the Old Yang Style. So people unfamiliar with this great martial art could in one volume see all its many aspects and gain a clearer understanding of the whole system.

Disclaimer

All training should be under the supervision of a qualified instructor of the World Taiji Boxing Association. All techniques, theories, training methods and any other information contained in any part of this book are presented for information purposes only! No liability whatsoever will be accepted, by the author or publisher for any damage or injuries that may arise from the use or misuse of information contained in this book.

Acknowledgment

Foreword

Introduction

Foreword
By Master Erle Montaigue

It gives me great pleasure to write the foreword for Paul Brecher's new book. Paul has been a student of mine since 1989 and in that time he has not only excelled at being a student, but also as a friend and now instructor. This book is a more advanced introductory book, however, it is written in such a way that the beginner right up to the advanced Taijiquan player will benefit from the contents. In particular it will give even the advanced student/instructor a totally different view to the common view held by most Tai Chi players.

Tai Chi ch'uan is not only one of the greatest and most deadly fighting systems ever invented but also one of the greatest self healing and medical arts having been derived from the ancient Chinese healing methods of acupuncture, bone and meridian manipulation. There are three areas that we must learn from our Taijiquan (Tai Chi) training and until these areas are learnt, we are only scraping the crust of Taijiquan.

Firstly we always begin with the Martial or Self-Defence area as this makes the healing way easier to understand. It is easier to learn how to use one's Qi in the fighting area first, then go on to the more subtle area of healing as we use exactly the same Qi for both. This is why this great healing arts is based upon the fighting system.

Once we are beginning to understand how to move correctly we find that our whole body and mind comes into a state of balance and we begin to feel well again. This is the 'Self Healing' area. We must of course pass through this area before going on to heal others using this art.

The third area of 'Medical Taijiquan' is the most difficult to understand and achieve because it involves much automatic response to sick people. Here we learn how to sub-consciously diagnose disease states and then to heal these states by either laying on of hands or simply being there! There is in fact an old saying from China which goes something like, (using some colloquial licence here) "When a sick person enters your space, if he or she is not healed by the time they reach your desk, then you ain't got it"! Which means that although we are able to learn all kinds of physical skills like acupuncture and massage etc, all of these mean nothing if you do not have anything internally to give out to the patient!

Paul has learnt all three areas of Taijiquan and has indeed become one of my top students because of his doggedness in asking incessant questions and wishing to gain the good oil, so-to-speak. I can recommend this book to all who would gain a better understanding of the Internal healing/martial arts.

Erle Montaigue
Master Degree, China

Introduction

The old way to spell the capitol of China is Peking, the new way is Beijing. It is the same with many words in this book to do with the internal arts. The old spelling is Tai chi, the new spelling is Taiji. Taoism is now Daoism and Wu tang Mountain is now Wu dang Mountain and Chi kung is now Qi gong and the Tan tien, the big energy centre in the belly is now called the Dan dien, I will be using the new way of spelling these words.

Taiji is actually an abbreviation of Taiji quan (Tai Chi Chuan), Taiji is the name of the Yin Yang diagram and quan means fist as in Chinese martial art. So Taiji quan means, the martial art based on the principles of Yin and Yang, or literally, Yin Yang Boxing.

Taiji has many benefits, it is a martial art for defeating opponents and it is also a type of Qi gong. Qi means energy and gong means achievement through hard work, so Qi gong means working with energy. Qi gong exercises are used to heal the body and defeat disease. In mainland China they say Taiji is the best Qi gong.

This book is about The Old Yang Style of Taiji which was named after its founder Yang Lu Chan 1799-1872. During his lifetime this style was recognised as being the ultimate fighting system in mainland China.

Taiji may have its origins in ancient China but it is as relevant today as it was then. People will always need ways of taking care of their health, defending themselves and finding out about their true nature.

If a person trains The Old Yang Style of Taiji as a martial art they will get its full healing benefits. If they train Taiji as a healing art only, they will get just a small improvement in their health. For this reason I will be going into great detail about the martial side of Taiji as well as the Qi gong healing aspects so that people can gain its full benefits.

This book explains both the martial and the healing, the physical and the spiritual because to maintain a balance in our lives all these areas must be explored.

If a person wishes not to have any martial component to their taiji then they can just learn the Old Yang Style Long Form and put into it all the Qi gong from the chapter on Internal Power.

In different chapters I mention different principles, these principles apply to the whole system and not just to the particular training method discussed in that specific chapter.

Chapter 1
The History of The Old Yang Style of Taiji

There are many different styles of taiji, some are named after the families that developed them and there are also more modern versions that are shortened or simplified versions or combinations of these styles. Each school of taiji has its own beliefs about the history of taiji and how it works for health and how it should be applied as a martial art. It is impossible for anyone to say that theirs is the true history or that their explanation of how the art works is the only correct way.

In this book I aim to contribute to the available literature on taiji with my present understanding based on my experience. This book is just one of many perspectives and I hope people who are training in taiji will find within it much useful and helpful information.

I believe the origins of taiji begin with Zhang San fen (also spelt Chang San Feng or Chang Sang Fen), who was born in 1247 or possibly 1279. From an early age he was taught martial arts by his father, he also studied the healing arts of acupuncture and qi gong.

Although the stories of his life are few one gets the impression of a man of great extremes he was a healer and a fighter and also a logical man who many people now regard as a Daoist mystic. He is depicted in paintings with a large forehead symbolic of great knowledge and wisdom but is also known to have personally killed dozens of people most of them in legitimate combat but a few in more questionable circumstances.

So we can see that the benefits of taiji directly reflect the qualities of its creator, it is very beneficial for improving ones health, it is outstanding for defeating opponents and is also a wonderful system for improving ones character and developing ones spiritual qualities.

Like his father Zhang San fen worked for the government, he was involved with the protection of trade routes, not just as an administrator, he would often ride with the caravans and defend them when they came under attack from bandit groups. These encounters were like small battles with both sides having archers, foot soldiers and mounted warriors, fighting with bows and arrows, spears and swords and daggers. So clearly Zhang's martial skill was based on practical reality, not philosophy and it also incorporated weapons skills and not just empty hand methods.

After the death of his parents he resigned from his government position and went to the Buddhist Shao lin temple to contemplate life and death. He spent ten years here further developing his martial arts skills, he exchanged knowledge with the monks who were also interested in martial arts training.

However he felt that his martial arts system and his spiritual development were still incomplete so he left the monastery and went on searching. It was at this time that Zhang decided to really go into great detail about how to use his knowledge of acupuncture to make his fighting skill more effective.

The way that acupuncture works is to insert the needles into acupuncture points on the acupuncture meridians in the direction that the qi (energy) flows to reinforce a weak part of the body. Or to insert the needles into acu-points against the direction that the qi flows to calm an overactive part of the body. The needles are also manipulated up and down whilst bieng rotated clock wise or anti clockwise to reinforce or reduce the qi flow. The direction depends on which hand you are using on which side of their body.

All the bodies muscles, bones and internal organs, the brain and nervous system can be healed by acupuncturing specific acupuncture points. Zhang san feng was convinced that he could use this same knowledge to adversely affect the opponents muscles, bones and internal organs, brain and nerve system in combat.

For example there is a point which acupuncturists use to reduce excessive heart activity, it is needled in the reducing direction to calm the heart. Zhang theorised that if a person were struck in the correct direction with sufficient force on this point it could cause the opponent to have reduced functional power of the heart. This would cause the blood pressure to drop and they would go unconscious, or if it was hit to hard they would have heart failure and die.

Zhang had a friend who was a magistrate and he had many convicts who had been tried and were awaiting execution. It was agreed that any of the criminals who could defeat Zhang could go free and so Zhang had his chance to experiment with his new ideas. One by one the convicts were released into the courtyard and told that if they could kill Zhang they would be freemen. So it was by this means that Zhang could test in a kill or be killed situation if his ideas worked.

Before he ran out of convicts he was able to confirm his theories, all the principles of acupuncture translated perfectly to fighting. He now knew that when he finally finished developing his own martial system that point striking would be an integral part of it. (The striking of acupuncture points has many different names I will be using the term Dim Mak.)

When Zhang was practising acupuncture to heal a patient he, like all good acupuncturists, sent his qi energy through the needles to heal them as well as allowing earth and universal energy to flow through him into them. When healing a patient the acupuncturist opens his heart and puts into the energy a healing intention. Zhang realised that in combat he needed to put a destructive intention into his qi to be able to affect the energy flow in his opponents bodies in an adverse way.Of course with dim mak some points work for purely anatomical reasons and no qi is needed but many of the points only work, or work with less effort, if qi is used in the strikes.

So Zhang developed a very advanced method to deliver the adverse qi into his opponents acupuncture points whilst fighting them, known as fa jin. Fa means to explosively release and jin is internal power, so fa jin are explosive energy strikes. One needs to have an excess of energy to be able to release some of it in a fa jin - dim mak strike. So Zhang decided that to increase his qi he would include advanced qi gong methods within his own emerging martial arts system so that his fa jin and dim mak would always work. Also he would have the great benifit of healing himself whilst he was training.

Adverse qi and healing qi are not two different types of energy it is the same energy but just given a different intention by the person who is transmitting it. Also the way in which it is emitted is different, for healing the energy is released by a gentle movement of the body. For fighting by a very sudden and violent shaking explosive movement of the body, fa jin. It is the same with acupuncture points and dim mak points, they are the same points being applied with the same theory but to bring about diffrent outcomes.

Zhang now retired to the Wu dang mountain range (there is still today a small temple dedicated to Zhang San feng on Wu dang, called Lang Mei, with a statue of him inside). It was here that he meditated and consolidated all his knowledge and experience and through his contact with the many local Daoist herbalists, healers, acupuncturists and qi gong practitioners was able to further develop his martial art and his spirit.

Zhang also studied the local martial arts being practised in the Wu dang area and felt a great affinity with them. He now had all the pieces of the puzzle he needed and spent many years combining all his knowledge of martial arts, qi gong and acupuncture to develop his own system. Many bandits and outlaws used to hide from the government troops in the Wu dang mountain range so Zhang also had plenty of opportunity to test out the martial effectiveness of his new system.

After many decades of refinement and evolution he eventually finished creating twelve forms known as The Twelve Qi Disruption Forms of Wu dang Mountain and their associated two person empty hand training methods known as The Twelve Hand Weapons of Wu dang and various weapons forms which contained all that he needed to continue his own development and to pass on to future generations the essence of his art. (It is highly probable that he began these forms but that it was his descendants / students over many generations who further refined and expanded on them.)

Zhang had created a martial art system for fighting that contained special qi gong exercises which would increase ones qi and invigorate its circulation around the body to improve health. The forms were also a type of moving meditation which had a spiritually transforming effect upon those who practised them.

It is not necessary to become a Buddhist (Yang Lu Chan was a Buddhist) or a Daoist to gain the benefits of taiji, all that one needs to do is train the system every day. This system created by Zhang san feng is now thought to be one of the earliest taiji styles or maybe even the very first.

All of the forms can be practised very slowly as self healing qi gong sequences or the movements can be fa jin dim mak strikes, to have true health and balance in ones life, doing both is best. The first nine of these forms contain hidden within them what are called qi disruption techniques. Each form has a different version of qi disruption concealed within it, these techniques are used in a fight as one is closing with the opponent. He has begun his attack and you move forwards to strike his torso, neck or head. It is at this point that qi disruption is used, one moves ones hands in a certain way over specific acupuncture meridians, just in front of their bodies, causing their qi to be disrupted in a particular way, each of the nine qi disruption techniques has a different effect.

For example one can disrupt the qi in his arms so that they lose some power and cannot be used to block your counterattacks as effectively. Or their qi can be drained from certain areas of their bodies making those areas more vulnerable to a fa jin dim mak attack. It is important to remember that learning qi disruption does not mean you no longer have to physically hit people or risk being hit yourself. It is just one extra interesting component of internal martial arts training.

Fighting is fighting, what makes taiji fighting different is in the details. For example like any other martial art you must practice hitting people, however in taiji we make the strikes fa jin strikes. Also like any other martial art we aim for the opponents weak points, however in taiji we aim to hit the acupuncture points on these same locations to get an even bigger effect. It is the same with qi disruption, if we can have a disruptive technique as part of our counter strikes it is an additional helpful tool but the essential thing like any other martial art is to hit them with massive force continuously from a position where they cannot hit you.

The way to best understand qi disruption is to make comparisons with other similar types of electromagnetic field effects. For example if a very strong magnet is brought close to a video or cassette tape they will be ruined. Or if a computer at the north pole is unshielded when the electromagnetic northern lights become very active the computer will have a systems failure. One is only able to disrupt anothers qi if ones own hands are highly charged like magnets and if ones body is free from any blocks that would restrict the qi flow. Also the qi disruption techniques must be done as fa jin to work. The last six of the Twelve Qi Disruption Forms contain within them a Yin and a Yang qi gong sequence. Each set is designed to achieve slightly different things but they will all heal the body and mind and have a spiritually transforming effect on whoever practices them.

Teachers of taiji, qi disruption and fa jin - dim mak should also know the antidote points which can heal the adverse affects and how to use these dim mak acupuncture points for healing. The knowledge and ability to both hurt and heal in the internal martial arts is a result of understanding acupuncture theory. So at the highest levels the martial arts are a healing art and an instructors job is not just to teach his students how to defeat opponents but to heal them and teach them how to heal themselves and others.

The Twelve Qi Disruption Forms of Wu Dang

Here is a very brief description of The Twelve Qi Disruption Forms

The Penetration Form

The First of the Qi Disruption Forms is used to penetrate the attacker's defences. This form increases the qi flow through the spleen meridian to strengthen and heal it. Also it strengthens the spine and the central nervous system and as a result makes ones reflexes sharper. The qi disruptive method in this form is applied with both hands waving horizontally in front of the the opponents face.

The Leaping Form

The Second Qi Disruptive Form as well as tonnifying the spleen also helps to balance the Qi flow between the upper and lower body. It is called the Leaping Form because we leap and twist around in the air when performing this form. It contains a Qi Disruption technique that brakes the qi flow between the upper and lower body in the opponent. The qi disruptive method in this form is applied with both hands waving vertically in front of the opponents torso.

The Eight Directions Form

The Third Qi Disruptive Form strengthens ones kidneys and improves the reflexes and contains a qi disruption technique that scatters the qi in the opponents head damaging their brain and their reflexes. It is called the Eight Directions Form because we are counter attacking opponents who come at us from all sides (the eight directions) . The qi disruptive method in this form is applied with one hand swiping horizontally in front of the opponents face.

The spiral Form

The Fourth Qi Disruptive Form also strengthens the kidneys and the nervous system and will improve ones reflexes. It contains many spiralling twisting movements which massage and heal the internal organs. The qi disruptive method in this form is a curving shape in front of the opponents face.

The Waving Form

The Fifth Qi Disruptive Form strengthens the lungs and can be used to heal many lung ailments. This form will increase ones internal power and contains a qi disruption technique that drains the qi from the opponents lungs. The qi disruptive method is a one hand cutting shape in front of the opponent.

The Closing Up Form

The Sixth Qi Disruptive Form strengthens ones heart and improves blood circulation to the brain. And it contains techniques that close down the opponents qi system. The qi disruptive method in this form is applied with both hands slicing vertically down the front of the torso and out to the sides.

The One Handed or Water Form

The Seventh Qi Disruptive Form contains qi gong which improves the flow of qi from the heavens above, down through you into the earth and from the earth up through you up to heaven. It opens up the meridians in the back and improves communication with the Spirit. The practice of this form makes it easier to have a good nights sleep. The qi disruptive method in this form can cause the opponent to go into a sleeplike state. The hand is brushed over the top of their head without quite touching.

The Ground or Earth Form

The Eighth Qi Disruptive Form contains qi gong which strengthens the stomach and develops a strong connection with the ground and the Earth Qi. It contains many spiralling twisting movements which massage and heal the internal organs. The qi disruptive method in this form is a cutting movement across the back of the opponents head.

The Wu Chi (emptiness) Form

The Ninth Qi Disruptive Form intergrates the whole body together and unifies the qi flow through all the meridians. This form balances all the different aspects of yin and yang qi and centres a person in their lower dan dien. It contains two powerful qi gong sets which heal the whole body by getting the qi to flow like a wave from the ground out through the palms of the hands. The qi disruptive method in this form drains all the yang energy from the opponent by moving the hand over their spine without quite touching.

The Stillness Form

The Tenth Qi Disruptive form concentrates on qi gong development. There are variations in the speed of ones movement in this form which help take ones training from the physical into the internal. This form emphasises the importance of having the movements of the hands a result of the qi circulating in the dan dien. One of the qi gong sets in this form develops the Vibrating Palm Fa jin, the other enables one to increase the flow of heaven qi through you into the ground and earth qi up through you to heaven and to store them in ones own dan dien.

The Prenatal Form

The Eleventh Qi Disruptive Form concentrates on qi gong development. This form is designed to intergrate the mind, body and spirit. To return us to something close to the state before we were born which is why it is called the Prenatal Form. This form strengthens the sexual energy and kidney qi as well as regulating ones weight.

The Finishing Form

The Twelfth Qi Disruptive Form increases ones qi to creat a youthful appearance, regulate ones weight and keep the kidneys power very strong as well as strengthening the liver and spleen. There are12 main parts to this form with each part working on one of the 12 main meridians in the body. The qi gong method in this form works directly on the dan dien balancing our Yin and Yang energy.

The Twelve Hand Weapons Forms Of Wu Dang

Here is a very brief description of The Twelve Hand Weapons Forms. In all these training methods the hands reflect the shape and activity of the weapon that the sequence is named after. These are two person training methods which teach fa jin, dim mak and continuous attack as well as sensitivity and awareness. They are a way of practising applying the qi disruption techniques and teach us how to know the intention of the attacker and as a result be in a position to attack him whilst being untouched by his attacks.

The Hammer Hand

We have the active hand in the shape of a fist known as the Hammer Hand and its attacking movements are like delivering hammer blows. We first hammer his arms and then his throat and temple and then his neck.

The Spear Hand

The hands are cut across the opponents eyes like a slicing spear tip and then they attack the neck. All Chinese spears have a loose flexibility so that the spear tip slashes back and forth, if this Spear Hand method is trained correctly we get the same effect with the fingertips.

The Sword Hand

The hands like the blade of a sword slice across his neck and we do a palm strike to his temple as if pounding the flat of the blade across the side of his head and then stab him in the neck with our fingertips as if they were the point of the sword.

The Plough Hand

Like digging up the ground we cut into the attackers arms and turn them away and then continue to plough into the opponents neck.

The Axe Hand

The hands are like axe blades which slice into the enemy, chopping him down with strikes to his neck and torso, felling him like a tree.

The Three Section Staff Hand

We use our hands and forearms like the Chinese implement for thrashing wheat or rice, the three section staff. We thrash the opponents arms and neck.

The Combination Weapon Hand

We use a combination of weapons, first we attack with the staff, then we use the hinge arm from the hammer and then the back of the hand like the flat of a sword blade and then a chop like an axe.

The Dart Hand

The dart is like a spear tip on a piece of string that is shot out at great speed, the hands duplicate this movement in their attacks.

The Drill Hand

We literally drill our way through the opponents defences as we counterattack.

The Spade Hand

We use our hands like a flat spade to slam the enemy with great force.

The Double Blade Hand

Both hands slice, cut and chop at the opponent.

The Tree Stump Puller Hand

We pull out the opponents joints like pulling out the stump of a plant. His wrist, elbow and shoulder are all dislocated.

Fortunately Zhang san fen taught his system to a few people before he died in 1368 and these Twelve Qi Disruption Forms of Wu Dang Mountain and Twelve Hand Weapons Forms later became transformed into what we today know as taiji.

There is a clan who are the direct lineage descendants of Zhang san feng and to this day still continue to practice The Twelve Qi Disruption Forms and Twelve Hand Weapons Forms and still live in the Wu dang mountain range in western China in the Liang village. The last great leader of this Wu dang style was Liang Shih Kan who was head of the village and died when he was over ninety years old in the late1990's.

He took over from Dong Kit yung who gave a long interview to a reporter from Beijing in 1973. In this interview he said the training in the forms begins at a very young age so that it is as natural as walking and that first we must learn to fight. Then we are able to move towards mastering ourselves and finally we can gain the inner mind. To begin this process takes twenty years and many years after that one can begin to master ones own destiny and inner spirit.

When asked about the history of taiji he said that one of the members of the Chen family was taught some of the Wu dang forms by a great Wu dang master and then many generations later Yang Lu Chan went to the Chen family village to learn what the Chen's were then practising. At this time another great master of the Wu dang system visited the Chen family village and began to teach both Yang Lu Chan and the Chen's more of the Wu dang forms. Yang Lu Chan left the Chen village with the Wu dang master and carried on studying with him. Many years later when Yang had mastered the Wu dang system and created his own style he returned to the Chen village and taught it to them.

(We learn from Wu yu hsiang (1812-1880) a student of Yang Lu Chan that the name of the first Wu dang master to teach the Chens was called Wang tsung yueh. The Tai Chi historian Wu tu nan went to the Chen family village in 1917 to interview Chen Hsin and was told by him that the name of the second Wu dang master who visited the Chen village was called Chiang Fa also spelt Zhiang Fa. In his 1921 Tai Chi book Hsu Yu sheng also confirms that the name of the person who taught the Chens was called Chiang Fa.)

Dong Kit yung talked at great length about the qi gong within the forms and about what makes a martial art internal. He explained the spiritual transmission of information energy from long dead teachers and concluded the interview by saying that the people who fight for money and glory have not mastered them selves.

Yang Lu Chan 1799-1872, lived near the Nan Guan (South Gate) of Kang Ping (Guang Ping) City in Yong Nian county in Hebei Province. He travelled around China with a bag over his shoulder and a spear in his hand. When ever he heard of a martial artist in the area he was passing through he would challenge them, often he fought with several people at once but always won. It is said that with every blow he drew blood and whenever he fought he took a life.

This may sound extreme to us today but in the troubled times that Yang Lu Chan lived martial artist worked as bodyguards for individuals and as protectors for the delivery of valuable goods for merchants and money for government tax collectors.

Work was dependent on ones reputation as an unbeaten fighter. Martial artists lived in a world of violence were no mercy was expected and non given. Yang Lu Chan was also a very accomplished practitioner of Traditional Chinese Herbal Medicine. So he was able to heal as well as fight which is the balanced approach all martial artists should have.

After his many triumphs all across China Yang Lu Chan arrived in the capitol, Beijing. Here he was challenged by the countries top fighters, on one occasion a champion fighter said to him, "Your style looks to soft to defeat anyone". Yang Lu Chan replied "Men are not made of wood or iron, they can all be defeated." when they fought Yang attacked instantly with the overwhelming force of fa jin dim mak and knocked the challenger unconscious with such severity that he dropped straight down where he stood and hit the ground hard as if he had fallen from a great height. Yang Lu Chan defeated all those who challenged him, he had a reputation as a the capitols champion fighter and was in great demand as a martial arts instructor, people refered to him as 'Yang of No Equal'.

To really understand why the martial art of Yang Lu Chan was so aggressive and violent we need to look at his life in its historical context. He lived in a time of discord and anarchy when many people carried knives and other weapons because they feared for their lives every day. In 1839 there was the Opium War against Britain and in1860 European troops attacked Beijing and the Emperor fled the city. Yang Lu Chan was in Beijing during this battle but it is unknown whether he and his martial arts brothers took part in the fighting. The Nien Rebellion of1852 raged on for many years and Yang Lu Chan's descendants were affected by the Boxer Rebellion of1898.

The greatest event that caused the most upheaval and violence began when Yang Lu Chan was fifty years old. A man called Hong Xiuquan had just finished spending ten years assembling his massive 'Taiping Heavenly Army of God'. Hong was convinced that he was the brother of Jesus and wanted to create a Christian state in China that he would call The New Jerusalem. He seized control of Nanjing city on the banks of the Yangzi river and used this as his base to fight the Imperial army of China. For fifteen years China was ripped apart by this civil war, twenty million people were killed in this conflict. So by the time Yang Lu Chan was sixty five years old he would have seen a lot of bloodshed and violence. In this time of such great suffering and turmoil it is understandable that he would have created a system that would enable him to survive. That he had many lethal and extreme methods to call upon would be a necessary in a country gripped by so much warfare.

The martial arts system which Yang Lu Chan developed was based on the Wu dang system which he continued to practice, his martial art is now known as The Old Yang Style of Taiji. Yang Lu Chan because of his fanatical single mindedness and continuous dedicated training became an unequalled fighter with incredible spiritual force. He passed on his system to his sons and died at the age of 73.

The Old Yang Style of Taiji

Here is a brief description of Yang Lu Chan's martial art system.

The Old Yang Style Long Form

The first thing one learns is The Old Yang Style Long Form, it contains all of the principles of the system, it is like a tree trunk and all the other forms and training methods are like branches that come from it. The Form is a continuous sequence of pre arranged fa jin dim mak moves. Fa jin, means moving in a fast and ferocious explosive way with the whole body shaking like a shark in a feeding frenzy.

Dim mak means striking the opponents acupuncture points to cause paralysis, collapse, unconsciousness or death. In The Old Yang Style only beginners practice the whole form slowly to learn correct movement, balance and coordination and to get the body to learn the moves. After that almost everything is fast and furious with explosive movements of great power. This is because it is a fighting style, we are training a martial art to defeat opponents, the health benefits are a side effect.

The Large San Sau

Next in the syllabus is The Large San Sau (Free Hands) Two Person Fighting Form, this prearranged fight sequence has an **A** and **B** side which fit together and enables the practitioners to get used to the close quarters ferocity and pressure of real combat. All possible combinations of strikes are used, punches and palm strikes, kicks and foot stomps, elbows, knees and shoulders. It also teaches the very important principle of attacking the attacker as he attacks you but getting your strike to hit him first. All the strikes are part of a continuous attack, there are no retreating moves in The Old Yang Style of Taiji,we always step forwards attacking the attacker.

The Pauchui

The Pauchui (Cannon Fist) Form, like everything else in this system is all fa jin dim mak, at first it seems to be similar to the Large San Sau but actually it contains what are known as the 'Hidden Applications' which are all designed to defeat grapplers by striking from no distance mainly to the neck using 'Non Techniques'. A technique is what the human thinking mind uses and a 'Non Technique' is produced by the reptile brain which is the survival mechanism that we need to activate to win the fight.

The Small San Sau

The Small San Sau Two Person Fighting Form, again its all fa jin dim mak in a short pre arranged fight sequence. This form teaches how to simultaneously counterattack the most common types of street attacks of straight punches, hook punches and uppercuts. It also teaches us how to headbutt correctly. It has connected to it twelve movements called ' The Mother Applications' , these are extra subconscious reflex attacking methods designed to encourage continuous attack. The reason for this overkill approach is that should you have to fight two opponents you want to be sure that the first one you hit will stay down. Because when you turn to take on the next one you don't want the first opponent to be able to get up and reattack you.

Lung Har Chuan

The Lung Har Chuan (Dragon Prawn Fist) are four separate fa jin dim mak abstract fighting methods which all eventually start to overlap with one another in a wide variety of combinations. This, like all taiji, is about learning a Way of moving that could have any number of applications, rather than training specific techniques. With these methods we move with the fluidity of a dragon and have great sensitivity in our hands like the feelers of a prawn.

The Twelve Circular Dim Mak Palms

The Twelve Circular Dim Mak Palms are to train us to intercept and apply multiple strikes from one fa jin movement. Each of these twelve methods is also a healing qi gong designed to rebalance the energy flow in a specific internal organ.

The Eight Pre emptive Attacking Methods

The circumstances in which these could be used would be if you faced multiple opponents and only by using pre emptive attacks could you have a chance of surviving. Or it could be that the person you are standing next to in a crowded bar is reaching for a knife and you have to strike first to stop him. Each of the Pre emptive Attacking Methods are a single fa jin move, attacking to the most deadly dim mak points, used from the covert taiji fighting stance.

The Da Lu

The Da Lu 'Four Corners ' teaches two people how to strike using the continuous rebound method with body checks and shoulder strikes, palm strikes, knees and forearm bars.

Single Pushing Hands and Double Pushing Hands

And last of all the glue which sticks the whole of the system together is Single Pushing Hands and Double Pushing Hands. They should really be called Striking Hands rather than Pushing Hands because in The Old Yang Style there are only strikes. We have no pushing or pulling, no throws or grappling techniques, only strikes. Every technique and Non technique, every type of attack and counter, every training method and principle that is in the system is within the Pushing Hands.

It gives us the sensitivity and connectivity that we need to know the opponent without him knowing us and the ability to not be where he is attacking whilst we attack him.

Weapons

The Old Yang style has a Long Sword and Hidden Dagger Form a Short Stick Form and a Short Stick San Sau (a two person fight sequence) and a Broadsword Form and a Spear Form. It also has knife attack methods and defence against knife attack when armed and unarmed. All the weapons forms like the empty hand forms contain fa jin dim mak. It is not entirely clear which weapons were originally from Wu dang and which were developed by the Yang family.

Yang Lu Chan was exceptionally harsh when he taught his sons, both his first son Yang Pan Hou 1837-1892 and his second son Yang Jian hou 1839-1917 tried to run away on many occasions but were always caught and brought back.

Yang Lu Chan insisted on incredibly high standards, on one occasion when Yang Pan Hou was attacked by a renowned wrestler and defeated him, his father would give him no praise. Yang Pan Hou describer how as the wrestler attacked he had leaped forwards with an explosive fa jin movement and unleashed a deadly series of dim mak strikes on the opponent, defeating him in an instant. Yang Lu chan shook his head in a dismissive and disappointed way and drew Yang Pan Hou's attention to a small tear in his sleeve caused by the wrestler. He should not have been able to even grab you, you must train harder, he said.

When Yang Pan Hou grew older he also trained his students with brutal force often beating them severely and occasionally breaking their bones. These extreme training methods and his insistence on heavy contact and realism in the training to achieve fighting ability resulted in him having very, very few students.

An incident is recorded about Yang Pan Hou which clearly conveys his ruthless and powerful martial ability and why he was so widely respected.

Yang Pan Hou was walking with his son when they were attacked by a martial artist of a different style, Yang Pan Hou counter attacked with a furious combination of fa jin dim mak attacks to the opponents head neck and throat. The opponent dropped dead on the spot. Yang Pan Hou carried on walking with his son and in an even manner as if nothing had happened he just said , 'The last sound he made was like a swallow singing.'

There is an interview with Chen fu kong who is the son of Chen fu wing, one of Yang Pan Hou's top students. When asked about Yang pan hou and his methods Chen fu kong goes into great detail because his father told him a great deal about Yang Pan hou and also trained Chen fu kong in The Old Yang Style the same way that Yang Pan hou trained him.

He said that Yang pan hou was only interested in the fighting and not the spiritual side of taiji and was very violent with his students. And that Yang Shao hu was much the same and trained as much with his uncle Yang Pan Hou as his father Yang Jian hou. Chen fu kong said that the emphasis in the single person forms and two person training methods was always on fajin without this one could not use taiji for fighting.

He went on to say that to knock the attacker out or kill them with the first move was how fa jin was used with an explosive punch to an acupuncture point delivered from as little as an inch or two away. The large san sau training was for getting used to taking punches and kicks and having heavy body contact in as realistic way as possible to be able to fight. It was also to teach timing and awareness, at first it was prearranged movements but eventually it became free fighting.

He said iron shirt qi gong was to protect the dim mak points from attack but it was only possible once the qi has sunk to the dan dien, this happens naturally once one is over thirty years old. Chen fu kong finished the interview by saying that he only teaches his son and four students who have been training with him for twenty years because not many understand his taiji way of fighting.

Yang Jian Hou had three sons, Shao Yuang, who died at an early age, his second son Yang Shao Hou (1862-1930) who kept the family style and taught it as it was originally intended, as a martial art. Last of all Yang Cheng Fu (1883-1936) the third son who only taught a very simplified version of the style for health. Yang Shao hu 1862-1930 learnt not only from his father Yang Jian Hou but also from his uncle Yang Pan Hou and up until the age of ten with his grandfather Yang Lu Chan.

Here is a description of how Yang Shao hu performed The Old Yang Style of Taiji.

Yang Shao hu was swift and powerful in delivering his blows and, with eyes blazing like torches, a grim smile on his face and roaring and howling as he darted back and forth, he was held in awe by others. The technical features of his taiji were: overcoming strong attacks with movements that appeared to be soft, adapting oneself to others movements and following up with quick attacks, using the motion of Sudden Connection Fa jin to defeat the opponent with surprise attacks. The hand movements included, catching, striking and capturing, injuring the attackers muscles and harming his bones, attacking the opponents acupuncture points and controlling his arteries and veins, using Continuous Fa jin and Sudden Connection Fa jin to strike the attacker down with lightning speed.

Yang Shao hu's most senior student was his second cousin Chang yiu chun (1896 -1986) who studied with him from 1911 until Yang Shao hu's death in 1930. In an interview Chang Yiu chun said Yang Shao hu had only three students because people could not handle his brutal training methods and beatings, at the end of a training session students would have blood on their shirts and many bruises and occasionally a broken bone.

Chang Yiu chun said his teachers form would be flowing like a river one moment and then explosive like a cannon shot the next. He said that the san sau training would have the moves out of order and was used in a hard, fast and brutal way to make it real. And that all the training had to be for fighting because only this would make the mind positive and strong and it was a strong mind which created the health benefit.

Training begins with set movements but eventually there are no set patterns so that the body and mind are united and spontaneous. After many years of training our natural instincts take over and we see the opponent as if we where an animal and so we can move as they move.

He explained that the pushing hands was about balance and yin yang theory and was a training method of attack and counterattack in an abstract way, it is not a competition. He said Pushing hands is to teach us to go forwards as he goes forwards just like it says in the classics. Pushing hands is for training sensitivity and building up the internal power not just for fighting, for fighting fa jin punch him in the head on an acupuncture point.

Chang yui chun went on to say that the inner mind must fa jin so you do not know you have done it and that whether we fa jin or have slow movement in the form, san sau or weapons sets it is all meditation. When asked about qi gong Chang Yiu chun replied that the qi gong was in the taiji and that it also helped to protect the body when attacked.

There were however some points that could not be protected just with qi gong and we have to be able to fight. Young people want to fight, middle aged people want to be able to defeat attackers and old people want to be healthy. (Chang Yiu chun was an acupuncturist, so he was also a healer and not just a fighter). He concluded by saying that after the whole system had been learnt and trained for many many years then the taiji was the mind movement and the internal would be activated and the taiji would teach us about the unknown.

Chang Yiu chun arrived in Australia by boat and Erle Montaigue, the head of The World Taiji Boxing Association, learnt The Old Yang Style Taiji System and the first few Qi Disruption Forms from him before Chang Yiu chun returned to China in 1986 were he died.

Erle Montaigue then travelled to and from the Wu dang mountain range were Liang Shih Kan the last great leader of this Wu dang style taught him the rest of The Twelve Qi Disruption Forms and The Twelve Hand Weapons of Wudang.

Erle Montaigue is the only western inheritor of both these remarkable systems direct from their original Chinese sources. He recommends that to understand The Old Yang Style Taiji System one also needs to learn The Twelve Qi Disruption Forms and Twelve Hand Weapons of Wudang because they are the origins of the system. We should remember that the Yang family practised the Wudang forms and Twelve Hand Weapons of Wudang along side their own family style.

I was first shown the Old Yang Style by Erle Montaigue in 1989 and later he taught me the Wu dang system. I now teach both these styles but knowing them and teaching them is only the beginning. I believe that it is only through regular daily training over many decades that the deeper qualities of these martial arts are revealed.

Zhang San fen 1279-1368
/
Wang tsung yueh
/
Zhiang Fa
/
Yang Lu Chan 1799-1872
/
Yang Pan hou 1837-1892
/
Yang Jian hou 1839-1917
/
Yang Shao hao 1862-1929
/
Chang Yiu chun 1896 -1986
/
Erle Montaigue 1949 -
/
Paul Brecher 1967-

The Taiji Classics
These are historical writings by the old masters, they are technical manuals written about variouse aspects of taiji which are helpful and interesting documents communicating many of the main principles of the style.

What the classics say about qi gong:
The elixir of life lies in the body, regulate the qi and the body will be well. Develop the body and mind, cultivate ones essence, qi and spirit. Train the martial and the spiritual, for self cultivation in taiji balance yin and yang to rejuvenate. The whole body is filled with qi, the changes of yin and yang move the qi. The qi spirals in the body like the coils of a snake. Inhale the qi to the dan dien, exhale to fa jin.

What the classics say about sensitivity training:
Remain internally reserved, contain hardness without expressing it, meet the opponent with softness causing him to know nothing of you. With the opponent rise and drop, speed up and slow down, evade and return, provoke and cease. Use adhering, connecting and following to attain this skill. Learn to interpret qi, use the eyes correctly, listen with the skin and remain balanced at all times. Increase your qi and keep your mind strong, drain the opponents qi and drain his strength. We are victorious, the opponent fails. You must understand the life and death hand techniques, you must understand the life and death acupuncture points. Attack the points so life is no more.

What the classics say about fighting:
Stick, connect and adhere to the opponent, draw the opponent in, attack with great force. Use spiral movements attack the opponents neck. Always maintain close contact but never grapple, use fa jin.

Be like a speeding horse destroying all in its path. Attack the opponents acupuncture points with the hand techniques of break, bend, beat and pound, press down, rub, push and grab, open and close, rise and fall. Applications for palm are strike down and forwards, applications for fingers are seek and stab the acupuncture points, applications for whole hand are break and drain opponents qi, applications for fist is to punch. Among punches there are, down and parry punch, below elbow punch, turn the body punch, upside down punch, open mountain punch, under leaf punch, reverse punch, power portion punch and rolling break punch. Remember the footwork follows the body.

Every move is an attack, destroy all in your path. Use elbow to take his life. Leave your opponent no room to escape, strike without mercy. The hand like a swift sword, slicing across the forehead or throat, send the opponent straight to hell.

What the classics say about moving with the opponent:
Strike the opponent when his attack is imminent but has not yet issued forth. The whole body must fa jin when attacked, this is an internal skill. To defeat the opponent one must be able to interpret his qi. Relate to the opponent with turn and exchange, advance and retreat. Know his hands forwards and backwards intention by gaze left but look right. Attacking the opponents blood vessels and acupuncture points and he will faint, forceful attacks on the death points terminate the opponents life.

What the classics say about ones own body movement:
Spine straight and vertical, sink the qi to the dan dien. Raise ones spirit and turn the hips continuously. Be flexible and soft, the body follows the qi, the qi follows the spirit.

Chapter 2
The Old Yang Style Long Form.

This form is the heart and soul of the whole system, it should be learnt before anything else because it contains within it all the ideas that we use later in the rest of our taiji. We learn about the correct posture and internal structure of the body, how to coordinate our movement in an integrated balanced way, how to fa jin and also we learn how to put all the different qi gongs in to our taiji movements. This form contains all the concepts we use to fight one opponent or multiple opponents and it also contains the framework for attacking an enemy armed with a knife. All the principles that we learn in this form are the same principles that we also use in the weapons forms.

If a person is only interested in taiji for health then this form is the one that they need. It has all the qi gong inside it (please see the chapter on internal power for more information on this) and if practised every day it can help to improve and maintain ones physical health and keep the mind and emotions more balanced. The way that the form works to heal the body is that if we have the body relaxed and flowing with a circular movement on the outside then internally the blood and qi will reflect this and be able to circulate smoothly on the inside.

The abdominal breathing and torso twisting in the form both help to massage all the internal organs increasing there ability to function more effectively. Also within this form the strikes are grouped together into sequences which emphasis the activation of specific acupuncture meridians to heal the internal organs that they connect to.

For example near the beginning of the form there is a series of strikes which are grouped together and called, grasp the birds tail, or grasp the sparrows tail. This sequence is used to maintain the health of the large intestine, or to heal it if it is affected by disease. The sequence known as waving hands like clouds is for the stomach and brush knee palm strike twist step is for the heart, high pat on horse is for the spleen, monkey strike for the liver, fan through the back for the small intestine, snake creeps down for the kidneys and mailed fist for the bladder etc

There is also a very subtle internal process of spiritual healing happening within the body that is so subtle that it can only be explained with a comparison. If we imagine that we are a glass of water but that the water is clouded with all our present and past thoughts emotions and experiences. So we find it hard to see clearly our true nature or the true nature of other people and the world around us.

If we practice taiji for twenty years then gradually all the internal turbulence reduces and all the particles settle to the bottom of the glass and the water becomes clear once again. So we have a greater clarity of vision in our lives and are able to see things as they really are.

With this form there are many things that happen which indicate that a person is practising their taiji correctly and gradually improving their health and developing their internal power. To begin with blocks in the energy become apparent as physical aches and shakes and mental discomfort, as the qi flows more strongly these are cleared away and there is a warm glow in the body and the mind is calm and clear.

As the flow of qi to the extremities increases so to does the flow of blood and the palms of the hands become red and blotchy with blood. The upper body becomes light and loose and the lower body becomes very sturdy and firm. The whole body feels as if it was made of warm, glowing, flowing liquid lead and the fingertips feel full and there is a tingling sensation in the finger tips.

There is a sense that the body is fixed in to the air around it and also it feels as if one were swimming through the air like it was a physical substance like water. The energy flow through the body also feels like water, one can feel a spiralling wave of energy moving through, this causes a very subtle physical ripple of movement. There is a movement from the feet to the hands and also a movement from the belly out to the hands feet and head. The result is that the hands are always waving, circling, spiralling and flowing.

As the qi level increases the hands also shake on the inside, it is only just visible on the outside, this is called the Vibrating Palm. The whole of the outside of the body also has a shell of vibrating qi around it, this is the defensive qi becoming highly activated. At the more advanced level we feel that by internalising all the qi gong the lower dan dien is activated and that all our movement comes from there. There is actually an experience of a very strong qi movement in the belly, not just an energy flow feeling but a sort of internal physical belly rotating sensation. It is this that actually creates all the internal qi gong and body movement.

When the yang energy has been built up sufficiently it causes several very extreme animalistic things to happen in the body and mind. The ears pull back, the eyes have a snake eyes stare and they also glare, there is a lot of expression on the face like a lion about to roar. And there is a grin which is not to do with happiness but rather a sort of knowing confidence. The back feels like it is rising up as if one were a cat about to catch a rat. The hands feel like claws and the fa jin shout is like a tigers roar as it leaps to the kill.

A more yin healing effect is that the qi creates a warm glow around the body and the hands go soft and warm and feel like they could heal some one if you placed your hands on them. One also feels an electromagnetic force field build up around the hands and body so that like magnets the fingers cannot touch each other, the hands and arms cannot touch the body and the legs cannot touch each other.

The qi coming from the hands looks like heat haze or out of focus air and the whole body has a nice gentle radiating glow around it, (when practising out side one can also see the same type of glow around the trees). Also one notices in the air around us a shimmer like a haze of golden glittering light, this seams to be more of a spiritual phenomenon rather than just energy.

We also have many alterations to our visual perception, our mind expands into our periphery vision which also expands beyond its natural scope. This is connected to an expanded awareness as if one was actually touching the air around oneself to a distance of some feet away from where one can actually physically reach.

There are also various unusual visual perceptions due to the increased qi flow through the eyes. One can see the qi trailing from the hands like the tail of a comet and there are also bright flashes. This particular experience has two different aspects, the first is the qi crossing over the optic nerve inside our heads and the second is to do with a type of cosmic radiation from deep space that we become aware of. Astronauts also report this phenomenon, it is apparently stronger when one is outside the protective cocoon of the earths atmosphere.

There is a higher level of sensation that is beyond feeling the qi as warm electromagnetism it is a feeling of no feeling. One is empty and transparent as air, the palms feel as if they were holding an empty space and after each expansion and contraction of the body on each movement there is a sensation of emptiness. The movements become less and less physical and more to do with energy and spirit. You feel like you are rising into the sky and sinking into the ground at the same time. It eventually gets to the point were you don't seam to be moving at all and have a sensation of being invisible to yourself.

To only practice taiji for health but not to do any of the contact combat training will bring a small increase in ones health. To do the whole system including all the two person training methods is what enables a person to gain the full health benefits. So this book will explain both the single person and two person forms and training methods so that whether a person is interested in taiji for fighting or for healing they will have all the information that they need.

To practice swinging a tennis racket or a golf club or a cricket bat but to never actually hit a ball would be strange. To practice drawing a bow but never loading and releasing an arrow would also be strange or to practice pointing a gun at a target but never loading a bullet and pulling the trigger would be unusual. With taiji it is the same, to learn the The Old Yang Style Long Form but never to pair up with a training partner and practice things like the Large san sau or Pushing hands would also be very strange.

The form is learnt as a solo form rather than a two person pre arranged fight sequence, which is two forms that fit together, like the Large san sau. However the applications of each of its movements are individually practised with a training partner. Some of the moves in the form are only done to one side but when we take the moves out the form and practice applying them with aggression on our aggressive training partners we of course practice both sides.

It is important for the training to be reasonably aggressive because we want to get used to the pressure, both physical and mental of a fight. Also we need to get used to functioning effectively even when we have a lot of Yang energy rushing around the body. Yang energy in western terms is a combination of fear, anxiety and anger all mixed together with adrenalin and enthusiasm. This creates a state of altered consciousness where what we sense and experience is sometimes enhanced and sometimes inhibited, speeded up or slowed down.

For example if a person is not trained to relax and exhale continuously as they strike repeatedly then their chest becomes constricted their blood pressure rises, their face goes red and their ability to hear and see is reduced. They enter a tunnel vision world of muted sounds and are unable to fight effectively.

On the other hand through the solo practice of the form people learn how to move in a relaxed flowing way combined with the appropriate breathing whilst releasing their energy into a series of continuous fa jin dim mak explosive strikes. So when the moves are trained with a partner or when we later learn the Large San Sau we are able to move fast and with clarity of both focused and peripheral vision.

One of the interesting things about the applications of the Old Yang style moves is that in the vast majority of cases it is possible to use the same attacking movement on the opponent whether they use their right or left hand and whether you are on the inside or outside of the arm.

The places that we strike to on the opponents body are all obvious target areas, head, eyes, neck, throat, solar plexus, groin and joints. We are aiming for these areas and specifically for acupuncture points on them. If we hit the point we get a very big result but even if we don't hit the point exactly, we still get a result because these are all very vulnerable areas of the body.

Almost all the moves in the Old Yang Style Long Form are counters against being attacked by two people, this is because often criminals work in pairs and we need to develop our ability to fight two people attacking from two directions at almost the same time.

The first mugger will attack you to not only try and defeat you but also to get your attention so that you are unaware of and unprepared for the attack from behind by the second assailant. So by training for this eventuality we are increasing our awareness and our chances of survival.

The attacks that we are training in this Long Form and all the other forms and training methods of the Old Yang Style system are very, very violent. They are so extreme that it takes many years of training to overcome the natural mental barriers that most people have about hurting some one else.

We are training to mame and kill this is still something that I personally am not totally comfortable with, mainly because I am an acupuncturist. So I spend my time healing people of injuries and illness and so teaching such a violent martial art as the Old Yang Style at times seems to contradict my medical work. Fortunately this style is also a qi gong healing system so it is balanced, it has both Yin (healing) and Yang (fighting).

The Old Yang Style is a martial art designed to attack and kill the opponent, we can alter it to make it non fatal but this reduce its effectiveness and so will increase the chances of us loosing the confrontation. Do you want to be killed by an opponent in a fight because you did'nt want to hurt the opponent ? Or do you want to live if that means taking his life ? If you are not prepared to fight to win, whatever it takes, then don't fight.

The Old Yang Style Long Form is split up into three sections, the first is relatively easy to perform. The second section is more demanding and the third section contains many complex and difficult movements. The vast majority of the moves in this form (and the whole system) are hand striking techniques there are only a few kicks. In the actual use of the system in reality we very rarely ever use any kicks, we do however have many ways to counter other people who try to kick us.

The hand strikes that we have in the form are, finger tip strikes, inside palm edge strikes, outside palm edge strikes, heel palm strikes, back hands, back fists, a move called squeeze in which we use our wrist to strike, we also have tiger claws and cobra snake strikes, hammer hands, hook hands, thumb strikes, penetration punches, eagle claws and the tiger paw punches. We also have elbow strikes, shoulders strikes and knee strikes, back kicks, upwards heel kicks, outside heel kicks, sweeping kicks and crescent kicks, front kicks and leaping double front kicks, the first kick is between his legs so he will lean forwards and the second is then into his exposed neck.

All of these techniques are side affects of the whole body fa jin movement. The blows are delivered with the power of the weight shift and waist turn, not just an extension of the arm or leg. And as we strike we also internaly sink so that our body weight is added to the force of the strike.

In the first section there are two big fa jin explosive moves and in the second section there are twelve big fa jin explosive moves so it is getting more energetic and more invigorated. The third and last section has another twelve big fa jin explosive moves and also has what looks like many leaping spinning knee techniques. A sort of curving axe kick, and many long low postures that demand a great deal of flexibility. So we can see that the form has been very carefully designed to warm the practitioner up in the first section so that they are made ready for the harder moves in the second and third sections.

The long low postures are to activate the acupuncture meridians in the legs, they do have martial uses but they are not practical fighting movements. The Old Yang Style System has a few moves that are like this, more for qi gong self healing rather than fighting. We still practice these moves because whether we are going to fight or not we still need to cultivate our health.

Every movement is designed to increase the qi flow to a different meridian to heal the internal organs that it connects to. So every part of the system that we train is a moving self healing qi gong sequence as well as a martial arts movement. By having fighting applications for the moves we are training our qi to rise up and defend the body and we are also training the mind to defeat opponents. The mind and the qi will also apply this attitude to defending the body from illness and disease and for fighting infection to keep us healthy.

Before we begin this or any other form we always stand in a still calm manner entering into a state known as wuji which means stillness or emptiness. This is symbolised by an empty circle which once we start moving then becomes filled with yin and yang and becomes the taiji diagram. The form begins relatively Yin (easy) and becomes more Yang (demanding and vigorous) but the last few moves of the form are always practised very very slowly as a type of warm down qi gong so that we finish feeling settled and calm rather than with a racing heart and ragged breath.

So we begin in wuji pass through all the different combinations of yin and yang and then once again return to wuji.

All the moves in the whole form are first learnt slowly so that every detail is clear and understood, it is easier for the mind and body to learn and memorise as a reflex action a move which is first learnt slowly. Also if we practice the form slow for the first few years it will help us to build up the qi for the explosive fa jin movements later. Also if we move slowly it is easier to be relaxed and if we are relaxed then we can have greater freedom of movement and an increased flow of blood and qi. Whenever I use the word relaxation or relax any where in the book the definition of of what I mean is that there is no additional unnecessary tension anywhere in the body, just the minimum we need to accomplish our objective. It is only possible to fa jin if we are relaxed, this is because with fa jin the body becomes like a giant elastic band, like rubber, soft springy and flexible. Whether one wants improved health, quicker reflex reactions or more martial fa jin internal power, relaxation is the key.

In the taji we learn to physically move without any additional unnecessary physical tension, so we are eventually able to be physically active without any unnecessary physical tension in our daily lives. In the taiji we also develop the ability to be mentally active with out any additional unnecessary mental tension and this also overspills into our day to day life. So in both our lives and our taji we can be more effective with less effort.

From a martial arts perspective if we are punching and have additional unnecessary tension in our muscles it is counter productive because tension is contraction and this will shorten the arm and make it pull towards us. We want to extend the arm away from us as we strike towards the opponent. So tension is not beneficial because we end up fighting against our selves when we should be fighting them.

Plus we want to avoid tension because it makes the blood vessels constrict which will restrict the flow of blood and qi. So if we are more relaxed we have more qi and blood flowing providing us with more power for our strikes. So we stay relaxed before the strike, during the striking movement and on contact with the opponent and after we have struck we are still relaxed. On contact we want to have the maximum amount of qi and blood packed into our hands so we have greater density in our strikes so we don't go tense at this point.

After the whole form has been learnt slowly, the next level is to do the big fa jin explosive movements on the specific moves that are intended for them. These moves are major energy release points in the form that we need to have otherwise we internally overheat. To really gain the greatest benefit for health and to develop the maximum power for fighting when we are practising the form as a solo set, we go Yin before these big Yang fa jin moves and after them we go Yin again.

To be Yin in this context means that before we fa jin we further relax and internally sink our body weight and coil ourselves up like a snake, winding the body up, before it strikes out and bites with its fangs extended.

If we do this then the fa jin is then more Yang, more explosive, more dynamic and devastating. The Yin state we enter after is slightly different than the one before the strike, we now become receptive and calm. The reason for having this particular state of being is that by releasing our energy in the fa jin we become for a fraction of a second empty and clear and are then refilled with more energy immediately after. So if we can be at ease during this moment we help to increase the benefits of being replenished and recharged with qi energy.

If a person is performing their fa jin correctly then they don't need to try and empty their minds to become calm and more Yin afterwards, the shear force of the energy rushing through them should blow them away, so that they are empty and receptive, this is known as being in a state of wuji.

There are two major ways of using the mind in meditation (all of taiji is meditation) one is to have the mind completely empty without even one thought passing through, this is yin. And the other is to have it full and concentrated on specific clearly defined tasks and not to have it deviate from this even a fraction, this is yang.

The Full-Yang and Empty-Yin of the mind is another example of how taiji is a way of bringing about perfect harmony within oneself on every level. We can use this understanding from our training in our practical applications of taiji for fighting.

Obviously at first our mind is full of things, where is the nearest weapon I can use? How many opponents are there? Am I in or out of view of the close circuit security cameras that are on every street corner? Has he got a weapon?

These are questions that one should not try and clear away because they are relevant and important, however there follows a moment just before the fight starts when the mind has to stop. We need to be in the Wuji state, open and receptive, empty, so we can be filled with a sense of the opponents intention, so that we can feel with our awareness what he is going to do just before he does it.

In a perfect world as soon as the person indicates that he is now an opponent by either giving a verbal threat of violence or by stepping into your personal space you would hit him and knock him out with a fa jin dim mak strike.

Unfortunately it is often the case that this moment is missed and he is ready for you to do something so it is vital that you don't. Rather you should now wait for him to do something, this will create a weakness that you can exploit.

The taiji classics explain how to win in this moment, we are told not to attack, we should let them attack and as they begin their move then we counterstrike, intercepting them and defeating them. The force of the contact will mentally and physically stun them because they are walking on to your counterattack.

They will be unable to adapt to the changed circumstances for a second because they had it in their mind that they were attacking you and now you are not where you were and they are being hit.

It is during this window of opportunity while they are coming to terms with the radically changed situation that you close the distance right up and then from a very close range you finish them off. The taiji finishing techniques are as final and fatal as a guillotine, they will never reattack again. This is ruthless but necessary, if there is a second opponent you just want to fight him. Not have your first opponent get up again and have to be fighting two people at the same time. So understanding Full and Empty in taiji is about storing and releasing the energy in fa jin and knowing when to be pro active and when to be responsive in a fight as a result of having the mind Full or Empty at the right moment.

So in the form we are constantly alternating our speed as our energy rises and falls, ebbs and flows. sometimes we go so slowly that to go through the whole form once might take us over one hour at other times at the advanced level when every move is a fa jin it might only take us fifteen minuets.

When we are using taiji for defeating opponents of course everything that we do is fast and furious like a golden eagle impacting with its prey at the end of a power dive or like a shark in a feeding frenzy with its quarry in its jaws, the shark shakes its whole body and tears apart its victim.

The advanced way of practising the form is when all the moves which are not big fa jin energy release explosions are done as small shaking fa jin. Big fa jin are done with a large slap step which we use to cover the distance between us and the opponent and small shaking fa jin moves cause us to have shuffle steps which we use when we have closed the distance and are standing next to the opponent. We use shuffle steps to adjust our position to the opponent, in fact it is his movement which causes us to be moved in to the most advantageous angle to attack him.

Only by training the whole of The Old Yang Style Taiji System can its unique way of fighting be understood. We learn how to close the distance, how to have their attack cause us to be moved by them into the correct position that enables us to hit them whilst being out of their reach. The feeling of closing the distance is like clapping your hands once, both hands move together, although you get there first. The feeling of moving with them is like shaking some ones hand, it is not clear who is shaking who because the movement is so balanced and coordinated.

Our training is designed so that the way they move causes us to be moved in an almost duplicate way. Imagine a man was holding a plank in the middle on his shoulder and a trouble maker came along and slammed one end of the plank. This would cause the man holding the plank to be spun around and of course through no fault of his, the trouble maker gets slammed in the back of the head by the other end of the plank. So it is the same in taiji, they move you and make you hit them !

There are certain specific qi gong postures and methods which we practice before the form to bring the energy up and out of the internal organs and into the blood, muscles, tendons and skin. And after we have finished we have more qi gong techniques to return the activated energy back to the internal organs and bones so that after our training we are left with a beneficial accumulation of energy rather than feeling drained and exhausted.

Like any other martial art or exercise system we are getting a benefit from invigorating the circulation of blood and energy around the body. This makes us all feel exhilarated, we don't end it there because if we just carried on expending energy every time we trained then over time the net result is that we are exhausting ourselves.

In taiji we always return the energy into the internal organs and condense it into the bones so that as we get older we get stronger and more powerful. Also the way fa jin moves our bodies it causes the qi to be sent out and then be returned to us. This is true for both the solo forms and the two person sets. Additionaly in a fight we also steal the opponents energy and add it to ours so as we fight they get weaker and we get stronger.

Taiji is a life time commitment that enhances our lives and can increase ones health to such a degree that we are able to resist many disease and so reach our full and complete lifespans. So we not only live to a grand old age but also enjoy good health right up to our last moment and so are able to make the most use of our time here on earth.

I like to look at it in a slightly simplified way by saying that we can split our life up into three parts. In our first thirty years we don't really know what is going on. We simply have not accumulated enough life experience to really have a broad view of the big picture. And then for the next thirty years we are working like crazy to look after our developing families.

So we are strong and healthy but without much free time and with a lot of responsibilities. The last thirty years have the potential to be our most rewarding, we have let our kids who are now thirty with families of their own go of and get on with it, we have accumulated sixty years of life experience and we have more free time.

This third of our lives may be our last but it should be as enjoyable as the other two. Unfortunately for many people poor health steals their opportunity to make the most of this last thirty years.

Now if we start practising taiji when we are children then when we begin the autumn of our years we would already have stored up sixty years of accumulated energy and internal power. So we can maintain our health and be mentally and physically active right up to the moment that we leave.

My choice of three thirty year periods was for convenience to illustrate a point, it could be that you were born with the potential for a life span longer than ninety years. Whether it is longer or shorter it is definitely more enjoyable if we have a healthy body and mind. The regular practice of The Old Yang Style Taiji System can contribute towards this, of course a balanced lifestyle and good diet are also essential. Everything you think, feel and do, are all contributory factors to your everyday health.

The Old Yang Style Long Form Posture Names

I have mostly used the traditional names of the movements and added the occasional explanation. The way I have numbered the moves means we end up with 258 but there are actually many more subtle smaller intermediary movements that I have not listed, so the true number is much greater.

The First Section
1. Tai Chi Commencement
2. Double Palm Circle To Left
3. Single Ward Off To The North
    Grasp Swallow's Tail To The East
4. Double Ward Off
5. Roll Back
6. Squeeze High
7. Block High Squeeze Low
8. Sit Back Ready, Fingers, Elbows, Palms with Tiger Claws
9. Sit Back ready, Cobra Snake Fingers
    Fishes In Eight
10. Elbow
11. Chop To The Corner
    Single Whip
12. Hook Hand
13. Yin Yang Palm Strike To The West
14. Spear Fingers Lift To The Heavens
15. Double Dragon Palm
16. Reverse Dragon Hands - FAJING
17. Play Guitar (Heel Stance, On Guard)
18. Roll Back
19. Shoulder Strike To The North
20. Stork Spreads Wings To The West
21. Lift Hands (Toe Stance, On Guard)
22. Spread The Weave
23. Brush Knee Right Palm Strike Twist Step
24. Play Guitar (Heel Stance On Guard)
25. Brush Knee Right Palm Strike Twist Step
26. Brush Knee Left Palm Strike Twist Step
27. Brush Knee Right Palm Strike Twist Step

28. Play Guitar (Heel Stance On Guard)
29. Brush Knee Right Palm Strike Twist Step
31. Hammer Hand, Cross Step and Parry
32. Double Low Hinge Block
33. Hammer Hand Punch - FAJING
34. Sit Back and Block
35. Double Palm Strike
36. Sit Back
37. Close Up and Cross Hands.

The Second Section
38. Brush Knee Right Palm Strike Twist Step to North West
39. Spread The Weave
40. Embrace Tiger Return To Mountain
    Grasp Swallow's Tail To The South East
41. Double Ward Off
42. Roll Back
43. Squeeze High
44. Block High Squeeze Low
45. Sit Back Ready, Fingers, Elbows, Palms with Tiger Claws
46. Sit Back ready, Cobra Snake Fingers
    Fishes In Eight
47. Elbow
48. Chop To The Corner
49. Guard The House
50. Fist Under Both Elbows (Double Tiger Paw Punch) - ONE FAJING
51. Step Back Repulse Monkey x 3 , Weight Forwards
52. Spear Through The Armour
53. Snake Wraps Around The Willow Tree
54. Middle Winding
55. Parting The Wild Horse's Mane
56. Spear Fingers Lift To The Heavens
57. Double Dragon Palm
58. Reverse Dragon Hands - FAJING
59. Play Guitar (Heel Stance On Guard)
60. Roll Back
61. Shoulder Strike To The North
62. Stork Spreads Wings To The North
63. Lift Hands (Toe Stance On Guard)
64. Spread the weave
65. Brush Knee Right Palm Strike Twist Step
66. Picking Up The Golden Needle From The Bottom Of The Sea
67. Fan Thru Neck
68. Turn and Attack to No.3
69. Right Penetration Punch, Sidefist, Tiger Paw Punch to Neck
70. Step Back and Left Penetration Punch, Sidefist, Tiger Paw Punch to Neck

71. Double Low Hinge Block
72. Hammer Hand Punch - FAJING
73. Press Points 4 and 7
    Grasp Swallow's Tail
74. Step With Right Foot and Squeeze High
75. Block High And Left Foot Cross Step
76. Step With Right Foot And Squeeze Low
77. Sit Back Ready, Fingers, Elbows, Palms with Tiger Claws
78. Sit Back ready, Cobra Snake Fingers
    Fishes In Eight
79. Elbow
80. Chop To The Corner
    Single Whip
81. Hook Hand
82. Yin Yang Palm Strike To The West
83. First Set Of Waving Hands Like Cloud x 4
    Single Whip
84. Hook Hand
85. Yin Yang Palm Strike To The West
86. Spear Hands Lift To The Heavens
87. High Pat On Horse (Toe Stance) To The West
88. Cover Strike and Chop To Rear
89. Twist sit and Spear Neck
90. Right Front Kick
91. High Pat On Horse To The West Weight Forwards
92. Cover Strike and Chop To Rear
93. Twist sit and Spear Neck
94. Left Front Kick
95. Turn Around, Anticlockwise Circle & Left Heel Kick
96. Brush Knee Right Palm Strike Twist Step
97. Brush Knee Left Palm Strike Twist Step
98. Hook Hand, Hammer Hand and Sweep Knee
99. Spiral Descending Punch
100. Cutting Hands
101. Leaping Double Front Kick
102. Carry Bread On The Arms To The Right and Hit Tiger On The Right
103. Little Hinge Block
104. Left Tiger Paw Punch To Neck - FAJING
105. Turn and Left Backfist - FAJING
106. Hammer down and Right Penetration Punch - FAJING
107. Carry Bread On The Arms To The Left and Hit Tiger On The Left
108. Little Hinge Block
109. Right Tiger paw Punch To Neck - FAJING
110. Turn and Right Backfist - FAJING
111. Hammer down and Left Penetration Punch - FAJING
112. Block and Clockwise Circle Right Heel Kick

113. Wind Through Ears (Double Penetration Punch to neck)
114. Attack Arm Down and Spear Hands
115. Kneel Down, Rise Up and Back Kick and Heel Kick
116. Take A Walk
117. Cross Kick To The South West
118. Knife Hands Cross Cut and Drop to Spear Fingers
119 Step Up Neck Break and Play Guitar (Left Heel Stance On Guard)
120. Left Penetration Punch Backfist
121. Tiger Paw Punch to neck
122. Double Low Hinge Block
123. Hammer Hand Punch - FAJING
124. Sit Back and Block
125. Double Palm Strike
126. Sit Back
127. Close Up and Cross Hands.

The Third Section
128. Brush Knee Right Palm Strike Twist Step to North West
129. Spread The Weave
130. Embrace Tiger Return To Mountain
    Grasp Swallow's Tail To The South East
131. Double Ward Off
132. Roll Back
133. Squeeze High
134. lock High Squeeze Low
135. Sit Back Ready, Fingers, Elbows, Palms with Tiger Claws
136. Sit Back ready, Cobra Snake Fingers
    Fishes In Eight
137. Elbow
138. Chop To The Corner
    Single Whip To North West
139. Hook Hand
140. Yin Yang Palm Strike
141. Diagonal Flying Posture X 3 (Shoulder Strike, Parting The Wild Horses Main)
142. Sit Back Cobra
143. Ward Off To The North
    Grasp Swallow's Tail
144. Double Ward Off To The East
145. Roll Back
146. Step Up Touch Point 7
147. Right Foot Step Forwards And Squeeze Low
148. Sit Back Ready, Fingers, Elbows, Palms with Tiger Claws
149. Sit Back ready, Cobra Snake Fingers
    Fishes In Eight
150. Elbow
151. Chop To The Corner

Single Whip
152. Hook Hand
153. Yin Yang Palm Strike To The West
154. Fair (or Jade) Lady Works The Shuttles To The 4 Corners
155. Sit Back Cobra
156. Ward Off To The North
Grasp Swallow's Tail
157. Double Ward Off To The East
158. Roll Back
159. Step Up and Touch Point 7
160. Right Foot Slap Step Forwards And Squeeze Low - FAJING
161. Sit Back Ready, Fingers, Elbows, Palms with Tiger Claws
162. Sit Back ready, Cobra Snake Fingers
Fishes In Eight
163. Elbow
164. Chop To The Corner
Single Whip
165. Hook Hand
166. Yin Yang Palm Strike To The West
167. Second Set Of Waving Hands Like Cloud x 4 (Cross Step)
Single Whip
168. Hook Hand
169. Yin Yang Palm Strike To The West
170. Snake Creeps Down with Upside down Hookhand
171. Golden Cockral stands On One Leg
172. Golden Cockral stands On One Leg With Tiger Claw
173. Tripping Repulse Monkey (weight forwards) x 1
174. Repulse Monkey (weight back) x 3
175. Snake Wraps Around The Willow Tree
176. Middle Winding
177. Parting The Wild Horse's Mane (Forearm attack to Neck)
178. Lift To The Heavens
179. Double Dragon Palm
180. Reverse Dragon Hands - FAJING
181. Play Guitar (Heel Stance On Guard)
182. Roll Back
183. Shoulder Strike
184. Stork Spreads Wings To The North
185. Lift Hands (Toe Stance On Guard)
186. Spread The Weave
187. Brush Knee Right Palm Strike Twist Step
188. Picking Up The Golden Needle From The Bottom Of The Sea
189. Fan Thru Neck
190. Turn Around Snake Spits Venom (also called Snake Sticks Out Tongue)
191. Right Penetration Punch, Sidefist, Tiger Paw Punch to Neck
192. Step Forwards and Left Penetration Punch, Sidefist, Tiger Paw Punch to Neck

193. Double Low Hinge Block
194. Hammer Hand Punch - FAJING
195. Press Points 4 and 7
    Grasp Swallow's Tail
196. Step With Right Foot and Squeeze High
197. Block High And Left Foot Cross Step
198. Step With Right Foot And Squeeze Low
199. Sit Back Ready, Fingers, Elbows, Palms with Tiger Claws
200. Sit Back ready, Cobra Snake Fingers
    Fishes In Eight
201. Elbow
202. Chop To The Corner
    Single Whip
203. Hook Hand
204. Yin Yang Palm Strike To The West
205. Third Set Of Waving Hands Like Cloud x 4 (Cross Step)
    Single Whip
206. Hook Hand
207. Yin Yang Palm Strike To The West
208. High Pat On Horse (Lift Left Knee)
209. Inspection Of Horse's Mouth To The West
210. Inspect Horse's Mouth To The North East
211. Sweep The Enemy
212. Dragon Whips His Tail (Crescent Kick)
213. Left Spear Hand - FAJING
214. Neck Break Punch
215. Press Points 4 and 7
216. Long Low Squeeze, Right Leg
217. Bending Backwards and Elbow, Left Leg
218. Bending Backwards and Hammer, Right Leg
219. Cross Block
220. Bending Backwards and Hammer, Left Leg - FAJING
221. Immortal Points The Way To Heaven
222. Spread The Wings
223. Ward Off To The South
224. Pigeon Flies to Heaven
225. Pounding The Mortar and Stirring The Cauldron
226. Intercept Elbow and Hammer
227. Cross Block, Drop, Elbow Break and Tiger Paw Punch to Neck
228. Pull Neck, Elbow Neck and Double Hammer Hands Attack- FAJING
229. Change Step and Left Hidden Hand Punch
230. Sleeves Dancing Like Plumb Blossoms
231. Double Tiger Paw Punch - ONE FAJING
232. Change Step and Right Hidden Hand Punch - FAJING
234. Press Points 4 and 7
    Grasp Swallow's Tail

235. Step With Right Foot and Squeeze High
236. Block High And Left Foot Cross Step
237. Step With Right Foot And Squeeze Low
238. Sit Back Ready, Fingers, Elbows, Palms with Tiger Claws
239. Sit Back ready, Cobra Snake Fingers
    Fishes In Eight
240. Elbow
241. Chop To The Corner
    Single Whip
242. Hook Hand
243. Yin Yang Palm Strike To The West
244. Intercept and Snake Creeps Down
245. Step Up To Form Seven Stars
246. Ride Tiger Back To Wu dang Mountain
247. Turn Around High Pat On Horse and Sweep The Lotus Root Kick
248. Spiralling Descending Left Hammer Hand Punch - FAJING
249. Bending Hinge and Counter Attack
250. Side Hammer
251. Draw Bow To Shoot Tiger
252. Cross Stamping Kick
253. Double Low Hinge Block
254. Hammer Hand Punch
255. Sit Back and Block
256. Double Palm Strike
257. Sit Back
258. Close Up and Cross Hands

End Of The Third Section

Chapter 3
The Large San Sau

The Large San Sau (Free Hands) Two Person Fighting Form is a prearranged fight sequence. It has an A and B side which fit together and enables the practitioners to get used to the close quarters ferocity and pressure of real combat. All possible combinations of strikes are used, punches and palm strikes, kicks and foot stomps, elbows, knees and shoulders. It also teaches the very important principle of attacking the attacker as he attacks you but getting your strike to hit him first.

All the strikes are part of a continuous attack, there are no retreating moves in The Old Yang Style of Taiji, we always step forwards attacking the attacker. On the rare occasions when we do have to step back we still strike out forwards towards them and always have a mental intention of being the aggressive attacker. To win with the least damage to ourselves we must always attack, go forwards and be mentally as well as physically on the offensive. And if we do have to go back we are still attacking forwards with our bodies and minds.

And if the enemy is controlling the space between you and you cannot get through with your attacks, then just attack his arms. Whenever his wrists come within range hit them again and again, until he can no longer use his arms because they are so damaged. Also because we have been hitting dim mak points on his wrists his whole body will have been drained and weakened.

In the large san sau we have a lot of heavy contact because we need to get desensitised to being hit. It would be disastrous if in the melee of a fight we were hit and started thinking 'oh no I have been hit' because we should not have the self perception of being the victim. We are focused on being the aggressor and dedicating our lives in that one moment to destroying the opponent. We do not think, we act, reverting to a type of ferocious reptilian survival instinct. We operate in the heat of a fight purely on reflex action, we do not think, when the switch is pressed we act. If someone makes the terrible mistake of thinking of attacking us we attack them with massive force.

In the large san sau each move is countered by either a Yin method like sliding forwards up the arm of the attackers striking limb and into a target point on their torso neck or head. The Yin way of countering is to have just enough contact to know what they are doing but without putting enough pressure onto them for them to be able to tell what your intentions are. Or we counter with a Yang method which is to hammer their attacking limb with such force that it becomes unusable and then a fraction of a second later to hit their torso head and neck. With this Yang method we are simply using our greater force to bring about victory. We have greater force even if they are stronger than us because of how we apply our fa jin dim mak power.

For an example I will use the parallel idea of a big battle, if the enemy had an army of one thousand men and we had just ten men then at first sight it looks like it would be impossible for us to win. However in taiji we do not face up against the opponent in a pitched battle, we are very selective about how we use our forces and how we target the opponents weakest points. What we would do is if he had his forces in ten groups of one hundred with a commander for each group, we would first use our ten men working as one group to assassinate one by one each of his ten commanders. So although overall we were outnumbered, in each of our ten strikes we had a ten to one advantage. Also we use our ten man group to target there field radio operators. Finally with the enemies army confused and without leadership or communications we then again use our ten man group to execute their general.

So a small force of ten defeats a stronger army of one thousand through superior strategy. This is how we use our taiji we concentrate all our available internal power resources and focus them on his weakest points. We strike to acupuncture points which paralyse his arms and legs, shut down his nervous system drain his energy and finally by targeting certain points on his neck and head we stop his brain communicating with its body and we have won.

In a situation in which you are fighting against an opponent who's face neck and head are unreachable for some reason and he is trying to attack you. Then attack his dim mak acupuncture points on his wrists and forearms. When ever he brings his arms up to strike out smash them repeatedly using the force of fa jin. This way you are stopping his attacks, weakening him and turning the tables so that when you go on the offensive he will have no defence.

In the Large san sau the timing of the moves enables most of the attacks to be deflected before they land so no one gets to seriously injured in the training. Some times a strike gets through, or there is no counter and a person gets hit. This is not a bad thing to have in ones training because it is necessary to desensitise oneself from the shock of being hit and of hitting someone else so that we can be effective in a fight. Sometimes when we train we intentionally let ourselves be hit on the dim mak points and as the years go by we let our training partner use greater and greater force, this is a major part of our 'iron shirt' training.

We are training with our martial arts brothers and sisters so of course we don't go for the kill so no one is going to suffer any serious injury, in training it is warm blooded because we know the people who we are training with. On the street it will be cold blooded and so on a regular basis we need to bring this feeling into our training. We need to practice with full speed, full power punches and kicks to get comfortable and familiar with the ferocity of real combat.

The Large San Sau

Here is a very simplified description of the **A** and **B** sides of The Old Yang Style Large San Sau. Instead of trying to describe the very intricate hand and foot work which enables us to avoid being hit by deflecting and moving forwards, I will just list the attacking moves which are easy to describe and can be recognised by most experienced martial artists.

A steps forwards and punches **B** in the solar plexus
B heel kicks to the outside of **A**'s knee and strikes his neck and floating rib
A kicks the inside of **B**'s knee and jabs his fingers into B's neck then punches **B** in the solar plexus
B counters with a back fist to **A**'s temple
A steps around him and elbows him in the ribs
B hits **A** in the back of the neck with a penetration punch
A elbows **B** in to the heart
B hits **A** with **A**'s own arm
A counters with a back fist to **B**'s head
B elbows **A** in to the heart
A hits **B** in the back of the head with a penetration punch
B backfists **A**'s eye
A counters with an open back hand to **B**'s neck
B uses double palm strike into **A**'s heart and lungs
A punches **B** in the solar plexus
B punches **A** in the solar plexus
A jabs his fingers into **B**'s neck then punches **B** in the jaw
B attacks **A**'s elbow joint
A leg sweeps **B** and goes to crushes his throat with a forearm strike
B attacks up into **A**'s ribs with his forearm
A counters with an elbow strike
B levers **A**'s elbow to snap it
A attacks with squeeze into **B**'s solar plexus
B uses double palm strike into **A**'s heart and lungs
A kicks **B** between the legs and then again in to his exposed throat
B then punches **A**'s floating rib
A leg sweeps **B** and goes to crushes his throat with a forearm strike
B palm strikes **A** up and under the chin
A jabs **B** in the neck and hammers down with his fist onto **B**'s chin
B heel kicks the inside of **A**'s knee
A attacks with squeeze into **B**'s solar plexus

B hammers down with his fist onto **A**'s elbow to snap it

A levers **B**'s elbow to snap it

B punches **A** in both sides of the neck almost simultaneously

A uses double palm strike into **B**'s heart and lungs

B punches **A** in the solar plexus

A hits **B** with a side palm into the ribs

B breaks **A**'s elbow

A uses double palm strike into **B**'s heart and lungs

B palm strikes **A**'s jaw

A uses double palm strike into **B**'s heart and lungs

B elbows **A** in the neck

A leg sweeps **B** and goes to crushes his throat with a forearm strike

B hammers down with his fist onto **A**'s elbow to snap it

A hits **B** in the back of the head with a penetration punch

B levers **A**'s elbow to snap it

A attacks with squeeze into **B**'s solar plexus

B attacks with squeeze into **A**'s ribs

A uses shoulder strike to **B**'s heart

B uses shoulder strike to **A**'s ribs

A uses his elbow to break **B**'s elbow

B knees **A** between the legs

A attacks the top of **B**'s spine

B heel kicks **A**'s inside knee

A attacks the top of **B**'s spine and then shoulders him in the ribs

B hammers down with his fist onto **A**'s elbow to snap it

A front kicks to **B**'s ribs

B attacks **A**'s kicking leg and uses double palm strike into **A**'s back

A uses the lotus kick to strike **B**'s kidneys

B attacks **A**'s kicking leg

A uses shoulder strike to **B**'s heart

B uses shoulder strike to **A**'s ribs

A attacks up into **B**'s ribs with his forearm

B body checks **A** and breaks his elbow

A attacks up into **B**'s ribs with his forearm on the other side

B body checks **A** and breaks his other elbow

A punches **B** in the solar plexus

B punches **A** between the legs

A heel kicks **B**'s knee and uses side palm into his ribs

B uses his own heel kick to kick **A**'s attacking leg

A breaks **B**'s elbow and uses the lotus kick to strike **B**'s kidneys

B attacks **A**'s leg and then strikes up into **A**'s ribs with his forearm

A palm heel strikes **B** between the legs

B strikes up into **A**'s ribs with his forearm

A punches **B** in the solar plexus

B jabs **A** in the neck and hammers his fist into **A**'s jaw

A palm strikes downwards into **B**'s heart

B uses a type of cobra strike to the back of **A**'s neck

A palm strikes downwards into **B**'s heart

B uses a type of cobra strike to the back of **A**'s neck on the other side

A palm strikes downwards into **B**'s heart

B kicks the inside of **A**'s knee

A attacks the top of **B**'s spine

B jabs his fingers into **A**'s throat

A breaks **B**'s elbow

B uses a rear hand cross punch to strike **A**'s ribs

A palm strikes near **B**'s scapular

B punches **A** in the solar plexus

A jabs his fingers into **B**'s throat

B kicks **A** between the legs and then again in to his exposed throat

A attacks the top of **B**'s spine

B attacks with double penetration punch

A attacks the top of **B**'s spine

That is a simplified description of the whole of The Old Yang Style Large San Sau Two Person Fighting Form. When listed fully A and B both have about 50 attacking movements each. Beginners practice the moves slowly to get the right timing and distance with technical accuracy on the use of each technique.

When practising the Large San Sau it is important that you do not intercept his attack before he has even begun it. Yes you know what he is going to do because it is a pre arranged sequence but he needs to be allowed to practice attacking. Also you need to practice intercepting an attack so let him do his move. Another thing which needs to be avoided is to just go through the moves, you need to be doing a move as a response to what he is doing to you, don't just run through the sequence. To make sure your training partner is aware and not just going through the motions, every now and then put in a move out of order.

Begin by having the A and B sides put together correctly and working properly at a slow pace. This is important because speed and power can always be added later but if there is not technical accuracy to begin with then however hard and fast you go, it will not work.

The next level up is when the whole sequence is done fast with more force, make sure your training partner can match the pressure you are putting him under. Work with each other to gradually over time increase the levels of speed and force being applied. Also as you increase the speed you are increasing your reflex reaction time, there is an inverse relationship between them. Faster attacks demand quicker responses, so as attack speed increases the time delay on the counter gets shorter until it is equal with the attack.

The pressure a person is physically put under in the large san sau is one of the ways that we develop our internal power. It is like two springs being compressed and released against each other to generate energy. We can develop our internal power in

The Old Yang Style Long Form by compressing and releasing our own internal springs but it will only take us up to a certain level. It is only through the Large San Sau and the single and double pushing hands that we can have our internal power taken up to the next level.

It is worth mentioning here the difference between internal power and external power. External power is mostly to do with the muscles and how they are each used individually. Internal power is more to do with the energy in the acupuncture meridians and the elastisity of the tendons and sinew, with the whole body all working together as a single unit.

With internal power we combine our body and energy with our mental intention. For example if you got a call that a member of your family was sick and desperately needed you but there was no transport to get to them and you had no other option but to run to get to them. Now there is a natural reason, your minds intention will be at one with your body and your energy will flow. And when you run to get to them it will be like you are flying.

Or if you lived in the wild mountains and your only way to survive the freezing deep snows of winter was to chop wood to burn as logs. Then when you are swinging that axe, again your minds intention and your body are at one and your energy will flow because there is a natural reason for what you are doing.

Now with taiji we have the most primordial natural phenomena in action, the body is under attack and must be defended. So we have the minds intention activated, we must defeat the opponent, and quite naturally a huge wellspring of energy will be released and the internal power of the body will increase incredibly. We will be developing our internal power because our body, mind and energy will all be naturally activated and coordinated without having to force it or make an effort. Also when we train the Large San Sau and the single and double pushing hands we are working with the pressure of people, so we will develop a way of generating and releasing natural human power.

Taiji trains the body to have a low centre of gravity and wiry elastic whole body power this is what it needs for good health and to defeat opponents. Health comes from the liver, heart, spleen lungs and kidneys and all the other internal organs. Taiji strengthens and heals the internal organs so we have not only a great martial art but also a great healing art.

The next level up of the Large San Sau is for each of the moves to be applied as fa jin, and the counter attack then becomes a fa jin rebound strike, which the other person then rebounds off etc. This more advanced way enables us to practice stealing the opponents energy and using it against them. This means that the force of his strike contributes to the power we have to hit him. We attack his attacking arm and bounce of it into our strike to his torso, neck or head. The harder his arm is the more rebound power we have.

For example if the tennis ball hits a wall it bounces back but if it hits the tennis net it just falls to the ground. So people who are tense when they fight give us an advantage because we can rebound off them and use that energy in our counterstrike and because we are relaxed the opponent cannot do this to us.

The most advanced way to train the Large San Sau is to have not just one application on each fa jin but to have two, three or four. So we then get the Large San Sau split up into lots of these small modules of concentrated explosive strikes. These modules are small self contained little fight sequences practised as bursts of fa jin explosive power. Although they are first learnt separately, they all eventually run into one another.

Here is the first module, all these moves happen in one burst of furious fa jin power.

A steps forwards and punches **B** in the solar plexus
B heel kicks **A's** knee and hook hand strikes his neck then punches his floating rib
A kicks the inside of **B's** knee and jabs his fingers into **B's** neck

At this advanced level we also alter the timing and distance of the movements so that we are much, much closer to the opponent for all these moves. This means that previously we would strike his punching arm at the wrist and then hit him in the head, now we strike his punching arm at the elbow. Also we used to strike his kicking leg at the ankle then attack his body, now we hit him at his knee. So by closing up the distance we are also reducing the respons time, so we are training to get in to attack harder and faster from closer.

All the modules are first practised in the correct order then as the years go by quite naturally when the time is right one finds that they are all similar to each other and it can quite easily happen in a different order. At first the A and B sides will put one module out of place by accident but it worked and the Large San Sau kept on going. Then they find that they had swapped sides whilst going through without realising where it happened. Then the modules happen in any order and it still works and then it becomes true San Sau, free fighting that was based on the Large San sau but is no longer limited to the original format.

This is what taiji as a fighting art is really all about at its highest level, a devastatingly effective way to counter attack from a close distance. This is good for us and unsettling for the opponent, he wants you to stay where you are and to remain at about his arms length punching distance so he can comfortably hit you. So what we do is to rush towards him with our devastating counterattack methods, closing the distance to be within his arms length.

Whether we are on the inside or outside of his lead or rear arm the principles we use remain the same, to be so close to him and already moving into his blind spot that he is at a major disadvantage, he has no room to punch us because we are inside his striking distance.

The best position is on the outside of the shoulder of his lead arm, we get there by moving forwards and to the side as he steps in to attack. We either hammer his lead arm which is a very Yang way and will shock his system or we slip around it, which is a very Yin way of getting to an advantages position without him knowing what we are doing. Once we get there we are are out of reach of his rear hand and can deliver a continuous series of fa jin dim mak strikes.

Whether we are on the outside of his lead arm or the outside of his rear arm we have the advantage of two hands against his one arm. So with one hand we are attacking his arm whilst with the other we are attacking his torso, head and neck. We then swap the hands over so that the attacking hand covers his arm and the other hand is then free to attack. We continue with this method as we move further around him. If we find ourselves on the inside of either of his arms we have plenty of methods for attacking from there or we have techniques to take us onto the out side of his arm.

We do not need to have arms length distance to punch across because getting the fist to travel over a distance to build up power is not how fa jin works. We are able to deliver ferocious punches, palm strikes, etc from just one inch with the use of the hips and waist shaking fa jin movement.

When a person reaches the higher levels of fa jin it is then possible to strike from no distance, just on touch contact. Fa jin will be explained in greater detail in a later chapter, if any one says they are doing The Old Yang Style of Taiji but has not got fa jin then its not the real thing because TAIJI IS FA JIN.

In the Large San Sau many of the same moves are used again and again by both sides. This is so that at an advanced level it becomes unclear who is A and who is B or where you are in the sequence and it evolves into full contact fa jin dim mak free fighting. San sau roughly translates as free hands meaning free fighting, which is what this prearranged sequence evolves into.

When we are eventually free fighting the fa jin dim mak strikes are almost all intercepted so no one is suffering to serious an injury. For those strikes which get through it must be remembered that even though there is contact, we are training with a partner, not fighting an opponent, so we are careful not to unnecessary harm them.

The Qi gong healing benefits of the Large San sau are all to do with pressure. The body is like a spring if left alone it goes stiff and rusts, if put under pressure, compressed and released, it stays springy and works for longer. So our training partner by attacking us is both physically and mentaly putting us under pressure. We become compressed like a spring, being given potential energy, which we then release in our counterattack. This force then puts the opponent under pressure and so it goes on. Both sides benefit from the development of this particular type of compress / release internal power.

The Large san sau is very long so we get a lot of pressure and of course we practice both sides so we are having created within ourselves a type of long lasting continuously powerful internal force. We are learning to be mentally and physically relaxed whilst being mentally and physically active under pressure this is a great skill for life not just martial arts.

We are cultivating a beneficial way of dealing with all of the problems we could encounter in life. To be able to be effective and relaxed whilst coping with extreme stress is a great achievement. To be mentally and physically active without any unnecessary mental or physical tension is a good way to avoid unnecessary stress related diseases.

Another benefit of training our energy to rise up and fight opponents is that it will more effectively also rises up to fight of illness and disease. So all taiji fight training is simultaneously enhancing body resistance and creating a strong conscious and sub conscious idea of winning by defeating the opponent whether it is human, viral or bacterial or even stress or adverse weather conditions.

Chapter 4
The Pauchui

The Pauchui (Cannon Fist) Form, like everything else in this system is all fa jin dim mak. For beginners it is a way for one person to practice the movements of the Large San Sau, first the A side then the B side as a single person form. It is traditional to learn the Pauchui Form before the Large San Sau is learnt.

The Pauchui Form has all movements of The Old Yang Style Long Form contained within it but they are mostly done in reverse. For example when we practice the posture known as Single Whip in the Long Form it is the left hand that does the palm strike and in the Pauchui form it is the right hand. So because this form balances the Long Form we do not need to practice the Long Form to the other side.

For beginners The Pauchui Form and The Old Yang Style Long Form appear to be very diffrent in the way that they are practiced. At an advanced level they can be trained in the same way and it is clear that they are variations on the same theme.

The moves of the Pauchui Form are first learnt slowly then fast, then each move is practised at the fa jin explosive pace, then a few moves are put together in each fa jin and last of all many moves are put together into one single fa jin module. So a students level of development in their learning of the Large san sau is paralleled by their level of development in the Pauchui.

The Pauchui (Cannon Fist) Form

A steps forwards and punches
A knee kick and neck jab and punch
A elbow
A elbow
A back fist
A penetration punch
A open back hand
A punches
A fingers jab to neck then punch jaw
A leg sweeps and forearm strike
A elbow
A squeeze
A double kicks
A leg sweeps with a forearm strike
A neck jabs and hammer
A squeeze
A attack to elbow to snap it
A double palm strike
A side palm
A double palm strike
A double palm strike
A leg sweep and forearm strike
A penetration punch
A squeeze
A shoulder strike
A elbow strike
A attack to the spine
A attacks to the spine and then shoulder strike
A front kicks
A lotus kick
A shoulder strike
A attack with forearm
A attack with forearm
A punch to solar plexus
A heel kick and side palm
A elbow break and lotus kick
A palm heel strike
A punch to the solar plexus
A palm strikes downwards
A palm strikes downwards
A palm strikes downwards
A attack to the top of the spine
A elbow break
A palm strike
A finger jab to throat

A attack to the top of the spine
B heel kick and punch
B back fist
B penetration punch
B palm strike
B elbow strike
B backfist
B double palm strike
B punch
B attack to the elbow joint
B forearm attack
B elbow joint attack
B double palm strike
B punch
B palm strike
B heel kick
B hammer fist
B double punch
B punch
B elbow break
B palm strike
B elbow
B hammer to elbow
B elbow break
B squeeze
B shoulder strike
B knee strike
B heel kick
B hammer to elbow
B double palm strike
B attack to leg
B shoulder strike
B body check and elbow break
B body check and elbow break
B punch
B heel kick
B forearm attack
B forearm attack
B jab to the neck and hammer
B cobra strike to neck
B cobra strike to neck
B seven stars attack to neck and kick
B finger jab to throat
B rear hand cross punch
B punch
B kick between the legs and then kick to throat

At an advanced level the Pauchui becomes something different, it contains what are known as the 'Hidden Applications' which are all designed to knock out or kill grapplers. We do this by striking from no distance mainly to the neck, head and throat using 'Non Techniques'. We do not have time for techniques because grapplers rush in very quickly and and there is only a brief moment to strike them down before they take you to the ground.

We train to destroy the grappler as he makes his move, we need to strike him so that he will drop straight down just where he is and be unconscious before he hits the ground. So we are still standing and therefore in a better position to take on the second assailant.

If we miss the moment and are taken down to the ground with them we can still hit them with the power of fa jin into dim mak points. This is because fa jin comes from the hips and waist shaking left, right, left or right, left, right and it works whether the feet are touching the ground or not.

If the opponent takes us to the ground we do not try and grapple or wrestle with them because this would keep us on the ground for a long time. Here we would be in a vulnerable position to an attack from a second opponent. We must defeat them as quickly as possible and get back on our feet. So if we are taken to the ground whilst he is trying to wrestle we are concentrating on delivering fa jin dim mak stikes to his eyes, neck and throat.

A technique is what the human thinking mind uses and a 'Non Technique' is a reflex action, a survival mechanism of the reptile brain. Humans have at the front of their skulls a human brain, behind that is the earlier type of brain, the mammal brain and right at the back is the reptile brain. It is through special methods in our taiji that we can enhance the activation of this reptile brain which is the key to our survival in a confrontation.

Humans think with their human brain, if we think about everything we do before we do it this will make our response slower, so we don't base our fighting methods on the workings of the human brain. The next one back is similar to other mammal's brains, it can think a bit but is mostly emotional, this is better because we feel before we think and so to work with this brain will make us faster. However the brain right at the back is the best one to work with, it connects directly into the top of the spinal cord, this is the reptile brain.

It has virtually no capacity to think or feel, its sole purpose is reflex reactions for survival. When a grappler attacks there is no time to think about what to do, we have to be effective in the moment without hesitating like a reptile, we do what is necessary to survive.

This is only possible with the non techniques that result from training the Pauchui as the Large San Sau first and then as the Hidden Applications many years later.

We are using reflex action and a way of moving that could have a wide variety of applications. We are not using our conscious minds with specific techniques, this would be to slow and our chosen technique might not not fit the rapidly changing situation.

Grapplers begin high then suddenly drop down low or other tactics like they will do a fake attack and then another and then the real one. They want us to commit to one technique in response to their provocation so that they can then quickly alter their move and catch us unawares and come in for the take down.

We are fortunate that all of our taji training is designed to make us move in a perfectly synchronised way with the opponent. So if they step forwards so do we and we hit them, very very hard, many many times.

A grappler usually finds that if he can close the distance a striker cannot hit them from close range but with taiji close range is our speciality. If they make the move we hit them, if they don't make a move but are within reach, we hit them. If they come in close and try to begin a fake attack we don't hold back and wait for the real attack, if we can touch them, we can hit them and if we can hit them once we can hit them again and again.

Most grapplers are trained to be able to take one or two blows as they move in but the blows they are trained to take are normal punches not fa jin dim mak strikes. Also the person who is throwing the punch usually has to pull there hand back before they throw it forwards towards the charging grappler. Whilst they are pulling it back and getting ready to punch the grappler has already got in and taken them down. If they just hit with their arm extending with no pull back to get ready they will be able to hit the grappler but their punch will have no power.

With taiji fa jin punches we do not have to pull back we strike forwards with our whole body movement, we have no getting ready idea before a strike, we just strike and because it is a fa jin it is immensely powerful. A fa jin strike to certain dim mak points on the neck will bring down an adult man, even if he has lots of muscles and a big body and weighs a lot and is very aggressive it makes no diffrence, he will still be brought down.

We also learn speacial ways of moving so that he does not knock us over as he is falling. We don't want to find ourselves on our backs on the ground stuck under the first unconsiouse opponent whilst the second one is moving in for his attack.

Also we need to remember that grappling and wrestling are a comparatively long process. There is the charge, the embrace, the take down, the manoeuvring for the dominant position and then the lock and control leading to a broken joint or a choke hold or a submission.

In taiji we do not follow this relatively long sequence, we just strike preemptively, or as they begin their attack or as they charge or as they embrace us or as we are going to the ground or when we arrive on the ground. So they have not yet got to the end point of there processes but we have already had six opportunities to incapacitate or kill them.

We must learnt the Large San Sau applications of the Pauchui first this gives our conscious minds a technique so that it is fixed with the idea that the moves have this use. Then after at least ten years of practice, totally separately from the San Sau, the Hidden Applications of the Pauchui are taught which become spontaneous reflex action Non Techniques. So we end up with different things happening on different levels at the same time, our conscious mind is doing a type of technique whilst our subconscious mind is doing a completely different Non Technique.

The Old Yang Style at first seems to be a physical system, we learn to move the body in a certain way to get powerful fa jin strikes. Then we become aware that the bodies movement is a side effect of the mobilisation of the qi. Then we eventually appreciate that the movement of the qi is a result of the our conscious and subconscious mind and at the most advanced level we our using Intention Force. This is explained in the chapter on Internal Power later in the book.

Chapter 5
The Small San Sau

The Small San Sau Two Person Fighting Form, is all fa jin dim mak in a short pre arranged fight sequence. This form teaches how to simultaneously counterattack the most common types of street attacks of straight punches, hook punches and uppercuts. The first half contains counterstrikes which we would use when we find ourselves on the inside of their attacking arm. The second half of this form contains ways for us to get on to the outside of their attacking arm.

The opponent first throws a right hook punch to the head, we turn a bit to our left and bring our arms up and out, they are just unlocked, this is a good structure which can take pressure and also transmit our fa jin power. Our left hand strikes his right wrist and our right hand a fraction of a second later chops him in the neck. Our left hand is on our centre line and our right arm has the elbow over our right knee. This alignment gives us a good structure and positions us perfectly to counterstrike them.

(We have the first mother application here, this will be explained at the end of the small san sau.)

The opponent next throws a left hook punch to the head, we turn our hips to the right, towards it and do the same counter on this side. He then attacks with another right hook and we turn back and repeat our first counter.

When we are counterattacking his first right hook punch we aware of his left hand but not looking at it. And when we have countered its attack we are aware of his right again but not looking at it. We use a special way of looking which is described in the taiji classics as 'Look left, gaze right and look right, gaze left.'

This means we have our eyes pointing to the left but our awareness is in our right periphery field of view and visa versa. So we are not looking at the opponent directly and don't make eye contact with him, during the fight.

Also before a fight this will help diffuse the situation because he might take this as you backing down and so not feel the need to prove himself by attacking. Or you could let him think this so he drops his guard and then hit him preemptively.

By putting our minds eye into our periphery view we activate the reptile brain, this gives us lightning reflexes, inhuman power and the essential dispassion necessary to maim and kill another human being. The human brain in most people has evolved to help other people, it is very hard to override this natural inclination and to intentionally harm someone. However the reptile brain does not have compassion or any other higher spiritual component, it is only concerned with survival.

I am a healer not a killer, I am an acupuncturist and a practitioner of Chinese Herbal Medicine, every day I am treating people and reinforcing that compassionate aspect of my human brain. If I had to rely on it in a fight I would lose.

I let my dispassionate inhuman reptile brain fight for me and do whatever is necessary to win. That is worth repeating, whatever is necessary to win. A fight is not a game nor is it a competition, you cannot hesitate for a second, you must fight first and think about it later. You must fight and win there is no other option, no second place and no silver medal. Remember the only way to win every time is to fight first, fight to win and fight to the finish, let your reptile mind take full control.

Now carrying on with the small san sau, after the attacker has thrown his right, left, right hook punch combination he then throws a low left uppercut into our right floating rib. We turn towards it, hammer it with both hands, step towards him and do a backfist with our left hand to the side of his jaw.

(We have the second mother application here, this will be explained at the end of the small san sau.)

All the counterattacks that we do are fa jin this means that all our hand movements come from the vigorous right, left, right or left, right, left rotation of our waist/ hips/ belly. This movement has such great power that not only does it move our hands but also our feet. All the steps we take are not a result of us using our leg muscles to lift the feet but a result of the centrifugal and centre petal rotational forces of the waist/ hips/ belly.

This movement at a high level is so forceful that it causes our feet to slam in to the ground one after the other almost like a little jump, it is however an involuntary movement not an intentional one. This slamming of the sole of the foot on to the ground releases a vast amount of Earth Energy up into the body which we can use for our strikes.

Next the attacker throws a low right uppercut into our left floating rib. We turn towards it, hammer it with both hands, step towards him and with our left hand we strike his torso and do a backfist with our right hand to the front of his jaw.

(We have the third mother application here, this will be explained at the end of the small san sau.)

Obviously if this was a real fight the attacker would have been defeated already but this sequence is a training method to build into the body various subconscious reflex actions, ways of moving and of course the ability to use fa jin and dim mak with great effect when under the continual pressure of a series of full power attacks.

Next the opponent throws a left uppercut to our right ribs so we turn towards it and first attack the vulnerable inside of his left elbow then his left wrist with both our hands, before we can do a counter he throws a right uppercut into our left ribs so we turn towards it and use both our hands to attack his right wrist and then we charge in and strike with both hands into his solar plexus using the hand posture called squeeze which is an attack with the back of our wrist.

(We have the fourth mother application here, this will be explained at the end of the small san sau.)

He then attacks with three hook punches to the head, right, left, right, we use the same counter on each of these. We turn towards it and our rear hand attacks his wrist and the lead hand attacks his vulnerable inside elbow joint and then with our lead hand we punch his jaw.

(We have the fifth mother application here, this will be explained at the end of the small san sau.)

We are able to punch his jaw with our lead hand very powerfully because we are striking with fa jin. If we did not have fa jin it is unlikely that a strike over such a short distance could have a great enough effect. In fact all of the Old Yang style counterattacks only work because they are done with fa jin and dim mak.

If a person tried to hit the opponent the way we do but had not practised the forms to build up the internal power for fa jin and did not study acupuncture to know the location and effect of the acupuncture points for dim mak then it is unlikely that their attack would work. So really if a person wants to have the incredible power and ability that can be gained from the Old Yang Style of Taiji they have to train the whole system over many years.

The opponent throws one more right hook, we turn towards it and with our left hand attack his right wrist and with our right hand in a Tigerpaw Fist we punch them in the throat.

(We have the six mother application here, this will be explained at the end of the small san sau.)

This way of striking is lethal, our whole body weight and our rotational power is being carried into our fist. To exaggerate this effect as we connect we sink down into our belly and into the ground so that our strike has more density power. Our fa jin rotation rushes the blood and qi energy from our bellies and torso into our hands so that they become dense and heavy. Also our internal sinking causes our body weight to manifest in our hands, when we add to this the foot slamming down into the ground for a shockwave rush of energy to rocket through our bodies and concentrate all of this overwhelming charge into one small vulnerable point on the opponent, in this case his throat, our victory and his defeat is unquestionable.

The sinking that we use on each contact with the opponent is an internal sensation, it is not just to do with bending the knees more. We need to relax the belly and all the muscles that are not one hundred percent necessary for the specific task that we are trying to achieve. We just let the muscles hang from our bones rather than keep them tense and holding the bones up. This martial concept for developing greater density with our strikes also has a side effect of a very important health benefit. The weight bearing effect of our muscles on our bones actually increases there density over time so that we are less likely to develop various types of brittle bone diseases that are a common feature of old age.

Another benifit for the bones comes from the high impact training aspects of many of the moves that we do in the Old Yang Style System. Our jumping forwards movements with the heavy landings and the heavy contact training in the two person methods increases bone density and protects us against the development of old age arthritus.

We have countered all the attacks so far in the small san sau on the inside and remained mostly right in front of the opponent. In many other parts of the Old Yang Style System we move forwards and out to the side so we are not directly confronting them. However here we are learning to build up our confidence and ability to hold our ground and counter attack when in the most adverse of circumstances. It may happen that you are trapped in a confined area and even if you wanted to move are unable to and have no option but to hold your ground and face the opponent front on and counter their frenzied attack.

In traditional martial arts there is a quality that is referred to as spirit, this has many meanings, one of which is to do with self confidence, tenacity and strength of will. It is a very important aspect of our nature that can be a deciding factor in a fight. It can provide you with that little extra bit of strength that is needed at the crucial moment to turn the tide of the encounter in your favour even when it seems as if all is lost. It can be the way to find a reserve of energy that gets you through a moment of extreme hardship.

The strengthening of ones spirit is only possible by practising being determined and showing great resolve under constant physical pressure. It is this which the small san sau training gives us the opportunity to develop as well as the obvious physical counter strikes.

In the beginning the attacker hammers his fists in to us with great force and we try to get our counter strikes working to have a good response to the blows that are reigning down upon us. And then very quickly the tide changes and it becomes clear that it is the attacker who is suffering because whenever he throws a punch we are hitting acupuncture points on his arms which cause him great local pain and make his arms go dead and more importantly they drain energy from his torso and head. So he feels progressively weaker and more vulnerable, in fact the harder he punches the greater the impact on his arms and the more he suffers.

So we have the situation where the person who appears to be the attacker is really the one sustaining the greatest amount of damage. If we were to ever land the neck and body blows with even just ten percent of our full power then the attacker would be felled in an instant. The main strikes that we use after the initial intercepting attack on his arms are so dangerous that we can only place them on to the target, just contacting but not striking with full force.

This is because fa jin power is enough to kill a person if you hit them almost anywhere in the head or neck anyway but we are targeting acupuncture points that are on the most weak and vulnerable areas. They are over major nerves and arteries, at certain vital joints and weak areas of the skull and of course many of them are used to carry the force of the fa jin along the meridian lines to various internal organs. So it is as if we went inside their body and physically punched their heart or brain, no one can survive this type of counter attack.

The reality of self defence is that we do not actually try and defend ourselves, if this is what we did then the attacker would continue to be the attacker and we would continue to be the victim, both physically and mentaly. The inevitable out come of this is that eventually one of his attacks get through we are weakened, he exploits this weakness and grinds us into the the ground where we are then kicked to death.

So the only way to stop this is to turn the tables, we must become the attacker, as soon as we are attacked or even as soon as we are threatened with attack we should not hesitate but go on the offensive, the only way to win is to reverse the rolls. They attack you and you don't defend yourself, you get out of the way of their attack and concentrate on attacking them.

This then gives you back the physical and mental advantage, it makes them the victim and us the victor. We use not only the correct techniques but also we now have the right frame of mind. We need to have a strong spirit, the will to win and to be outraged that we have been attacked and to use our reflex reaction training to immediately take the fight to them. To put them on their back leg, to seize the initiative and crush them like a bug.

Taiji should really be thought of not as a system of self defence but as a style designed to defeat opponents. This slight difference in words makes a huge difference when it is our strategy on the field of battle.

The best form of defence is attack, the best mind set is one concentrated on defeating the enemy and the Old Yang Style is a system which cultivates a personality able to achieve these things.

The next thing that we do in the small san sau is to use our left hand to grab his right wrist and we turn our bodies so that he is twisted around and we are on the outside of his right arm. We grab and lift his right arm with our right hand, then step to the outside of his body and then we strike with the back of our left hand into his liver.

(We have the seventh mother application here, this will be explained at the end of the small san sau.)

The position we now find ourselves in is really the optimum location, close to his torso, on the outside of his lead arm, having just hit him once. We are now in the perfect situation to follow up our initial counterattack with more and more strikes as we move round behind him. This is what we do when we practice the mother applications of the small san sau. I will go into more detail about these when I have finished explaining the rest of the main part of the small san sau.

The opponent next throws a left hook punch to our head, so we now do the same move on the other side. We grab his left wrist with our right hand twist our waist to spin him around , lift his arm up with our left hand as we step forwards with our right foot to the outside of his left arm and with the back of our right hand we strike him in the spleen.

We are able to grab his punching hand because it is a swinging hook that he is not pulling back but trying to follow through with it. Obviously if it was a very quick short sharp straight jab it would be very hard to catch.

He then charges in to strangle us, we raise our arms up and to the sides to deflect his hands to our outside whilst we are also pulling him on to us. As he gets close enough we head butt him in his temple which is the thinnest part of the skull with the front corner of our head, which is one of the thickest parts of the skull. This way he sustains massive injuries and we are not damaging ourselves. Also we hit him from the side with the movement of our head coming from a vigorous rotation of our hips like all our other fa jin movements.

His head goes back and his chest is exposed at this point so, as always, we seize the advantage, step forwards and do a double palm strike into his heart and lungs.

(We have the eighth mother application here, this will be explained at the end of the small san sau.)

The blows land one after the other not at the same time, this is how we strike with all our dim mak techniques. Whenever they throw a punch if we are using the Yang method we hit what is called a set up point first on their wrist or forearm or if they kick we hit near the ankle or knee.

This drains the energy from their body making them weak and vulnerable to our main attack which lands a split second later. Also it brings their mind into their extremities so that their energy will also be there and not protecting their torso neck and head. All the fa jin strikes to the arm and leg dim mak points are so intense that for a moment whatever their intention was, they are unable to do any thing and it is in this moment, when they are in a state of shock, that we hit them with the main strikes.

The main strike or strikes are delivered to the torso, head and neck, these are the ones that have the most devastating effect on the opponent, (although it is possible to incapacitate the opponent with some of the extremities strikes if you have enough energy). The time delay between the strike to their arm and the strike to their body is only a fraction of a second and when we hit their body with a series of strikes it is again also one after the other, never two at the same time.

With a Yin method of counterstrike we would slip forwards only just touching their arm or leg with a very slight brushing movement that they can only barley feel. Sometimes we have no contact on the extremities at all, we just avoid being where they are attacking and angle forwards and to the side and concentrate on crushing the dim mak points on their head and neck.

So if we are small and they are big with a huge build, strong muscles and powerful punches it is not relevant. We are not facing them and fighting them we are avoiding a direct confrontation, sliding by them and hitting their brain, nervous system and draining their energy.

Next in the small san sau they block our double palm strike upwards and try and do a tiger paw punch up under our left arm. We attack their wrist with both our hands spin them around step forwards to the outside and hit them with a heel palm strike to the temple.

(We have the ninth mother application here, this will be explained at the end of the small san sau.)

They then throw a left uppercut and we have the same response on this side. Our counter to their next right punch is to land heavily on their wrist and elbow again spin them and this time attack with a hook hand strike to various points on the side of their rib cage.

(We have the tenth mother application here, this will be explained at the end of the small san sau.)

The side of the rib cage has very little muscle protection and fa jin strikes here go straight through into the internal organs. They throw a left and we have a very similar counter to their ribs on the other side. Next they throw another right this time we take their arm and drop our body weight onto the joint to break the elbow whilst we use our spear fingers to their neck.

(We have the eleventh mother application here, this will be explained at the end of the small san sau.)

Their next high left right left punch combination we counter with a hook hand intercept and follow though with a palm strike counter to their temple.

(We have the twelfth mother application here, this will be explained at the end of the small san sau.)

With our palm strikes we first have the hand in a Yin shape, this is when the yin meridians on the inside of the palm and arm are compressed and the yang meridians on the back of the hand and outside of the arm are stretched. By the time we have connected with the target the hand has become Yang shaped, this is when the yang meridians on the back of the hand and outside of the arm have become compressed and the yin meridians on the palm are stretched.

On contact we flatten out our cupped palm shape and release our adverse qi from the palm of our hand into the opponent. We are moving our whole body in a circular way which causes the massive release of Yang energy to arc from the palms of our hands and curve up and over their heads penetrating into their skull to send a curving destructive shockwave of electrical energy deep into their brain.

There is an even more advanced aspect to fa jin dim mak strikes, it is easy to describe but takes a few years to really master because it involves a combination of several different internal movements. What we do is to move our qi in our lower dan dien energy centre in the lower belly in such a way that it causes our hand to have three ways of moving all at the same time. To an observer who does not know what to look for we will have appeared to have just done a sort of straight strike. However the hand is simultaneously moving up and down as it goes forward, like a wave. It is also spiralling like the head of a drill end on a power drill. And it is also shaking backwards and forwards as it goes forwards like a hammer drill. These three are all combined together and are very very small internal movements which cannot be seen however the effect on the opponent is terminal.
The last moves of the small san sau, he rushes in to strangle or grapple us, we hit him with both hands in the jaw, pull him down onto a rising knee to his neck or temple and then finish him off with strikes to points just above both his collar bones.

This brings us to the end of the main small san sau fighting form, one person has been able to practice continuous attack with regular punches and the other has been able to practice the Old Yang Style way of simultaneous counter attack.

The Small San sau has connected to it twelve movements called ' The Mother Applications', these are extra subconscious reflex attacking methods designed to encourage continuous attack. The reason for this overkill approach is that should you have to fight two opponents you want to be sure that the first one you hit will stay down. Because when you turn to take on the next one you don't want the first opponent to be able to get up and reattack you.

The Small San Sau Mother Applications

Indicated in the text is where each of the mother applications are and here is a list of what they are.

1. The hand that attacked his neck now reattacks with an elbow then another chop and then circles around his neck and pulls his head in close into a head lock type neck break against the torso. The grab hand now releases and slams down onto his twisted and exposed neck.

2. We reattack his jaw with an open back hand and then using the same hand twist his head into another head lock neck break and then punch him in the throat with a tigerpaw fist. To finish the punching hand now slams down onto his twisted and exposed neck.

3. The hand which backfisted his jaw now attacks his elbow, using the leverage of one hand on his wrist and the other on his elbow we tear this elbow joint and then the hand that was by his elbow snakes around his arm and attacks his neck. We then kick his leg out from under him and as he is dropped onto his back we land on top of him and knee him in the groin as we thrust our fingers through his eyes.

4. With our right arm we elbow him straight into the solar plexus then we do a tigerpaw punch to the same area with our left tiger paw fist. To finish we strike with our right elbow upwards across his ribs into his heart.

5. Tiger paw fist into the throat with the left then palm strike with the right to the neck and then palm strike with the left to the head.

6. Strike up into the jaw with the right which then slams down into their collar bone and then snake around their neck and pull them onto your elbow strike to the throat.

7. The hand that lifted their arm up now also strikes to their ribs with a palm strike, then we step behind them and do another palm strike with our other hand into their kidneys. Then we stomp on the back of their knee and as they go down we strike across their heart and solar plexus.

8. We cut down the sides of their neck with the knife edge of our hands, first on one side and then the other, then we attack up into their jaw with our hook hands, first on one side and then the other.

9. We grab his hair and pull his head one way and then the other as we slice across his eyes with our other hand. We then drag his head down as we thrust our fingers into his throat.

10. We lift his arm up with a hook hand attack and then tigerpaw punch up under his arm, then twist his arm down to break it and levering his whole body around we finish by elbowing him in the back of the head.

11. We attack to his neck and head pull him down on to our rising knee to his face and then finish with an elbow into the top of his head.

12. We grab and twist his arm down and strike above the elbow to break it and levering his whole body around we then strike him in the neck. We then palm strike down into the area of his collar bone as we heel kick into the back of his knee and as he goes down we hit him in the neck one more time.

We never practice the mother applications within the small san sau form, they are always practised separately. The reason for this is that as we go through the small san sau form when we get to the parts where each of the mother applications are, we really want to do them as follow on sequences, to the move we are practising. However by not doing them they remain as subconscious impulses, so when we are in real combat, where there is no time for conscious decisions these mother applications just happen as spontaneous subconscious reflex actions.

The mother applications are very extreme and when we are thinking with our human brains we do understandably find some of them unacceptable. However our reptile brain needs ferocious moves to defend the body with when our lives are at risk. It is also important that we remember that The Old Yang Style of Taiji comes from China in a time of violent anarchy and civil war.

Although most people who read this book are unlikely to find themselves in a civil war or in a country reduced to violent anarchy we still need to train for the possibility of being attacked when going about our daily lives. Where ever you live there is always the possibility of violent crime, hopefully it will never touch your life and obviously one should not live in a paranoid world of fear of attack but even though we hope for the best, it is always worth being prepared for the worst.

We read in the newspapers on a regular basis stories of innocent people being fatally stabbed in the streets, or even criminals attacking people in their own homes. There are also many incidents in which no weapons were used and the victim was literally kicked to death in the street by one or more people. You can't rely on the general public to come and help you and the police may not get there in time, so if no body is going to save you, then you have to train to save your self. The Old Yang Style Of Taiji may have an overkill approach but better to have it and not need it than not have it when you need it.

Chapter 6
Lung Har Chuan

The Lung Har Chuan (Dragon Prawn Boxing) are four separate Fa jin - Dim Mak abstract fighting methods which all eventually start to overlap with one another in a wide variety of combinations. This, like all taiji, is about learning a Way of moving that could have any number of applications, rather than training specific techniques. These four ways of moving are taught with certain applications but it is obvious that they could be applied in many different ways.

It is good to experiment with all the possibilities but we always have to remember that we are practising a training method to develop a way of moving not just a sequence of techniques. Lung Har Chuan has been designed a specific way to develop specific subconscious reflex actions and the original methods should always be taught not the variations.

There is a test used by therapists designed to find out more about a persons mind. A piece of blotting paper has some ink put on it and it is then folded in half so that there is a symmetrical pattern. At first glance people might say that the pattern looks like a butterfly or a leaf. And then when encouraged to say more they might see more things, a face or a tree etc

What people very quickly lose sight of is that it is just an abstract pattern, it is not a butterfly/leaf/ face/tree or anything else. It is the same with all of our taiji, the moves are just abstract patterns which have been very cleverly designed to always enable us to be able to fa jin in to a dim mak point but not with a specific one off technique.

Taiji is not a technique based system it is a way of moving that could be applied in a wide variety of ways. It is not a style that relies on having to use this technique to counter that specific attack rather it is a way of moving which is flowing and variable and can transform as the situation develops. Our intercept to their attack moulds itself to them as the distance closes.

The way of moving has been created so skilfully that we can use the same move on the inside or outside of the opponents front or rear hand and at the intercept distance of his wrist or elbow and it will always work.

The name of these four little training methods is Dragon Prawn. The idea of being like a dragon is to be flowing and to use sinew power, to twist and turn and to have our movement like a creature that is part of nature. People have separated them selves from nature to protect themselves from its harsh and extreme dangers but in the process have also become so distant that they forget that they are part of nature. It is as a result of this that people have lost touch with their own true nature and so need a system like taiji to find themselves and their natural place in the world.

The idea of being like a prawn is because we curve our back into a C shape like a prawn is curved, this will release the yang survival qi that is stored in the spine. When a silver back mountain gorilla attacks it also curves its spine into a C shape, when a shark goes into a feeding frenzy it also has a C back.

When a cornered cat is about to attack it to makes a C shaped back. We can initiate the release of our own yang survival energy power with this same internal posture. Animals go wild with incredible ferocity to defend themselves and their home and family, we to have this untapped potential and all the things we do in our taiji training are designed to bring out this dormant survival mechanism.

The Vertical Method
The first Dragon Prawn is called the vertical method and it shows us how to win when we are on the inside of both their arms and they throw a lead hand followed by a rear cross. We attack their wrists and elbows on the insides of the joints and then chop into their neck and throat.

The Lateral Method
The second Dragon Prawn is called the lateral method and is used to defeat two quick straight jabs, we intercept on the outside of both arms and then hit them in the back of the head.

The Willow Tree Method
The third Dragon Prawn is called the willow tree method, as they throw their front hand punch we move up the outside of their arm and turn their body away from us as we move further around behind them. Striking them repeatedly around the eyes neck and back of the head.

The Continual Method
The fourth Dragon Prawn is called the continual method and is an intercept to the outside or inside of a lead hand or rear hand punch, we attack their spine and throat as we kick their knee.

All of these methods are practised continually, so for example on the first one he will attack one-two. We do the inside counter and he attacks again with the same combination and we do the same counter.

Then we do the same with the second and third and fourth Dragon Prawn methods until everything is flowing smoothly and we are moving in tune with them with the correct footwork.

Taiji footwork in general is designed to get us round behind the opponent. We don't step back when we counter, we attack forwards, we move around them staying close and controlling them as we continue to strike from very close range. We are so close that they find it very hard to counter or get any power for their punches. We have immense power from our fa jin at no distance and all our training is designed to make us comfortable at working at very close range.

If we are ever forced to step back then even as we are going back we are striking forwards. For example as we move back we turn and release a devastating penetration punch which will be doubly effective because they are walking on to it or we kick them between the legs. Whatever we do it reflects the fact that even if we are appearing to step back we are still on the offensive with the intention of defeating the opponent.

The final stage in Dragon Prawn training is for them to throw wildly random punches in strange combinations and for us to be able to use all the Lung Har Chuan Dragon Prawn Boxing methods as continuous flowing smooth counter attacks. We get to the level where we are moving with them in perfect harmony almost as if their were pieces of string tied to us and them. So as they move it moves us, there are in fact connections but they are not string they are qi. We subconsciously feel their qi and attune to it and so are able to effortlessly move with them.

Chapter 7
The Twelve Circular Dim Mak Palms

These twelve circular dim mak palms are what are known as fighting methods. This means that there is no flowing exchange of attacks and counters between you and your training partner like in the large and small san sau or single and double pushing hands or the da lu or lung har chuan.

With these dim mak palms the training partner attacks with a one two punch combination and before they are half way through the first punch we hit them with four, five or six strikes from one fa jin movement. We are training to smash the opponent repeatedly and unrelentingly as our first move. There is no exchange of blows, no fair fight, we just slam down on our internal accelerator and go to top speed right at the beginning.

We are able to go from a passive state into a berserk frenzy because we know how to trigger the reptile brain into an instant survival reaction. Many martial artists have to keep themselves in an always ready state and so cannot relax and enjoy their lives. We do have a level of awareness in operation so that we don't walk unknowingly into danger but apart from that, we are in general, not in a state of being constantly fired up. So we don't burn ourselves up and are able to enjoy our day to to day lives in a relatively easy going way.

When something happens we can go to one hundred percent action in a split second because the reptile brain needs no warm up, it is always subconsciously on, it just needs to be accessed.

When a person has reached an advanced level of understanding and ability about the Old Yang Style of Taiji then the frenzy of the reptile brains survival mechanism becomes part of our fa jin which contains all the ideas in this book. So how and where we move to and how we move and how we interact with the opponent and how we strike and where we strike are all part of the same single way of doing things which is what the training is ultimately trying to cultivate. The training of the taiji system with all its forms and training methods is all designed to eventually get us into the Way of Taiji.

With these twelve fighting methods we do not allow the opponent any chance to recover or adapt or roll with the blow. The moves are designed to attack his response movements, for example with the first dim mak palm he begins his first punch and we move forwards and to the side and attack his face with a tiger paw punch. This will cause his head to go back and the next two strikes are to the exposed neck and underside of the jaw, this will cause his torso to arch back pushing his rib cage forwards. So our final strike is to his now extended floating rib.

So his first attack brought him close enough to us to strike him, and our strike presented us with another target and so on. The fa jin is so explosively fast that all our strikes happen in the blink of an eye and cannot be avoided. To use a military metaphor, instead of trying to hit the opponent many times very quickly which would be like using a machine gun and shooting towards him and having the shots land closer and closer until we hit him. Instead we use fa jin which is like throwing a grenade in his face which is timed to detonate on arrival.

A man might see the line of bullets kicking up the earth as the rapid machine gun fire approached him and have a chance to dive for cover but when a grenade explodes in front of his face and the shrapnel flies in all directions at once there is no escape.

This description of the difference between trying to hit someone many times quickly and a fa jin move which contains many almost simultaneous strikes is very graphic and unsettling. It is an image from battle which most civilians are never exposed to. However if an individual who is going about their everyday life is attacked in the street or in their own home by an intruder, for them the intensity of the experience turns it into that persons own private war.

The assailant may have picked up a kitchen knife and be about to attack you with that as a weapon, it is not a bayonet but the injuries will be just the same. So if we think along the same strategic lines for a one to one confrontation as we would for a war we can have more effective tactics.

It is standard military doctrine that when peace negotiations have broken down and the enemy has begun mobilising his forces for his attack that if we preempt him and attack his ships before they leave port and attack his planes before they take to the sky we increase our chances of winning. And that is what we are training to do with these twelve fighting methods.

We have tried to avoid a conflict but now it is about to begin, the enemy is beginning to launch his first attack and so we bomb him. We use overwhelming force to ensure victory. Again this is the standard tactics of warfare, to concentrate your forces in such a way that at any one place on the battlefield our troops and their available firepower are superior in quality and quantity to the opponent whenever possible.

So he begins to hit us with one punch delivered from the local power of his upper body and we hit him six times with our whole body fa jin power on his most vulnerable dim mak points. And we keep on going forwards with our angled attack. If you imagine that you are on the point of the letter V and the opponent is in front of you then as he steps straight ahead to hit you . You move out along either the left or right branch of the V and you will find yourself in a position where you are not where he was attacking and are in an excellent position to attack him.

You step as he steps, it is not necessary to be faster than him, just as fast is enough. This is because as his punch lands it is hitting empty air, the point of the V that you once occupied and your strike lands at the same time on his neck. So we are winning because we have a better strategy, he could be younger and stronger but this does not matter because we are not trying to be stronger.

He can hit the point in space that we used to be standing in as hard and fast as he likes. We are not there, we are using all our fa jin power not to block him but to hit him. We don't want to block him, we want him to carry on coming forwards so that he is bringing his vulnerable dim mak points on his head, neck and throat closer to us so we can hit them.

If we are going to use these twelve dim mak palms for fight training then as the years go by we slowly increase the amount of contact that we have with our training partner. This is one of the best ways to build up the use of the yang defensive qi for 'iron shirt' in combat.

To train these forms in solo practice for fighting, practice number 1 first at explosive fa jin pace on alternate sides stepping forwards each time until you have done it nine times on each side. Then do the the same with number 2 etc.

If these twelve dim mak palms are going to be used as a self healing qi gung set then practice number 1 first, twelve times slowly. Then number 2 twelve times slowly and then number 3 etc.

If the qi builds up and makes you fa jin just let it. It is very important from a self healing perspective never to try and make fa jin happen because you will just be expending qi and getting weaker. True fa jin must be when the qi has built up so much that it makes you fa jin to clear away an excess. An unbalanced excess of qi is just as damaging to ones health as a deficiency of qi.

The Twelve Dim Mak Palms

1. Snake Hands.

Fighting.
We intercept their attack and counter with a Tiger Paw Punch to the face, a Reverse Tiger Paw Punch to the neck and then finish them with a Side Palm to the jaw and a Heal Palm Strike to the ribs.

Qi gung.
When used for Qi gung this form strengthens the heart and blood vessels and increases the flow of qi in the palms of the hands to heal others.

2. Straight Hands.

Fighting.
We intercept their attack and counter with Spear Fingers to the neck and Heal Palm Strike to the ribs. Then we use a penetration Punch to the head followed by a change step Back Fist and Palm Strike to the jaw.

Qi gung.
When used for Qi gung this form creates calmness and stillness strengthens the small intestines and blood vessels.

3. Changing Hands.

Fighting.
We intercept their attack and counter with Tiger Claw to the eyes followed by a Back Hand slam to the face, then Spear Fingers to the throat and a change step Side Palm to the jaw.

Qi gung.
When used for Qi gung this form strengthens the kidneys and bones and marrow and helps to give us the strength of will we need to be able to change our lives.

4. Throwing Hands.

Fighting.
We intercept their attack and strike to the inside of their attacking arm at the wrist and elbow, we then spin them around as we forearm bar their throat then Tiger Claw their eyes and finish them with neck break and Knife Edge Palm across the throat.

Qi gung.
When used for Qi gung this form strengthens the Bladder and it enables us to transformation Essence to Energy to Spirit in the Lower Dan Dien.

5. Waving Hands.

Fighting.
We intercept their attack and counter with Cobra Strike to the eyes followed by Tiger Paw punch to the throat, change step Side Palm to the jaw and then Tiger Claw to the collar bone followed by Monkey Strike to the head and Side Palm and Reverse Elbow Strike to the ribs.

Qi gung.
When used for Qi gung this form strengthens the Pericardium and blood vessels and it helps improve our concentration.

6. Breaking Hand.

Fighting.
We intercept their attack and counter with Cobra Strike to the eyes followed by Side Palm to the jaw, then we use the hand sign known as Immortal Points the Way to Heaven to attack their neck and throat and we then finish them with a change step neck break.

Qi gung.
When used for Qi gung this form strengthens the Triple Warmer Meridian and it helps to fire up the Dan Dien.

7. Willow Hand.

Fighting.
We intercept their attack and strike the out side of their attacking arm we then separate their elbow and attack their jaw with a Side Palm and we then finish them with a double changing neck break.

Qi gung.
When used for Qi gung this form strengthens the Gallbladder and muscles and sinews and it helps to mix all the different energies in the body.

8. Hammer Hand.

Fighting.
We intercept their attack and strike to the inside of their attacking arm at the wrist and elbow, we then counter their second attack with a Cobra Strike to their eyes, we then separate their elbow and finish them with a Hammer Hand Strike to the ribs.

Qi gung.
When used for Qi gung this form strengthens the Liver and the muscles and tendons and it will calm the central nervous system and help in the recovery from illness.

9. Bumping Cutting Hand.

Fighting.
We intercept their attack and counter with Double Spear to the neck followed by Double Hook Hand Strikes to the jaw and then Double Descending Knife Edge Palm to the neck. We hit their neck with a Side Palm and spin them into a neck break head lock and finish them with a descending Knife Edge Palm Strike across the throat.

Qi gung.
When used for Qi gung this form strengthens the Lungs and the Skin and hair and it makes the body more Yang and can help to recover from chronic fatigue syndrome.

10. Small Circle Hand.

Fighting.
We intercept their attack and counter with a Tiger Paw Punch to the face then we pull their head down on to a rising Tiger Paw Punch to the throat. We then hit them in the temple with a Heel Palm and then use a Side Palm to bring their head over to the other side where we then pull them down onto our rising knee and strike them in the back of the neck.

Qi gung.
When used for Qi gung this form strengthens the Large Intestine and it aligns the energy of the three Dan Diens.

11. Eagle Shape Hand.

Fighting.
We intercept their attack and strike to the inside of their attacking arm at the wrist and elbow, we then use the Eagle Claw to first strike upwards across their face and then downwards and finish them with a reverse Elbow Strike.

Qi gung.
When used for Qi gung this form strengthens the Stomach and the muscles and it increases the defensive energy so that the body is more resistant to disease.

12. Double Changing Palm.

Fighting.
We intercept their attack and counter with a Tiger Paw Punch to the face then we use an outside turning Tiger Paw punch to the neck combined with Spear Finger to the eyes followed by an inside turning Tiger Paw punch combined with Spear Finger to the eyes. We then use Double Tiger Paw Punch to both sides of the neck and then pull their head onto a forearm strike to the throat.

Qi gung.

When used for Qi gung this form strengthens the Spleen and muscles and it balances Yin and Yang in the body.

One of the important things to be aware of is that all of these twelve methods are lead hand attacks, so we have less distance to cover to the target than if we punched from the rear hand. Also the opponent has less time to react from our lead hand strike and we get to land the first blow. We can then hit him again whilst he is trying to recover from the first strike.

The Twelve Circular Dim Mak Palms are to train us to intercept and apply multiple strikes from one fa jin movement. At an advanced level of course we don't intercept, we attack first.

Chapter 8
The Eight Pre emptive Attacking Methods

The Eight Pre emptive Attacking Methods devised by Chang yui chun and the extra ninth one created by Erle Montaigue work exceptionaly well. The circumstances in which they could be used would be if you faced multiple opponents and only by using pre emptive attacks could you have a chance of surviving. Or it could be that you are in a crowded place and cannot get away and the person you are standing next to is reaching for a knife to stab you and you have to strike first to stop him.

We do have speacial ways of defeating an opponent with a knife once it is in motion but there is a very high probability of getting cut in the proccess. So whenever possible it is best to defeat him before the knife is unleashed. Each of the Preemptive Attacking Methods are used from the covert taiji fighting stance and are a single fa jin move, attacking to the most deadly dim mak points.

The circular nature of the movement in these methods and in the whole system are to improve our health by invigorating the circulation. For fighting the circular way of moving is the most natural and effective. This circular way of moving means the out and back movement of our hands created by the hip/waist/belly turn provides us with a continual intercept and attack ability.

The out and back movement of the hand is not along a straight line, it is really a very stretched oval shape. Some of our taiji punches may look like straight punches but are in fact spiralling corkscrew type movements.

Inside us the blood and qi is circulating in our lower dan dien and our whole body, balancing and healing us and creating great internal power.

The circular way of moving the body causes our hands and feet to move in a rolling circular way. This fits perfectly with moving around the opponents body which is made of circular shapes. When we hit their dim mak points it is with a strike that spirals clockwise or anti clockwise to reduce the qi in their bodies causing them to collapse, be knocked unconscious or die.

The Nine Pre emptive Attacking Methods

1. Dog Fist, Elbow, Cutting Hand, Double Tiger paw.

2. Reverse Dog Fist, Cutting Hand, Elbow.

3. Hammer Punch, Palm Strike, Penertration Punch.

4. Penertration Punch, Palm Strike, Cutting Hand.

5. Palm Strike, Cutting Hand, Hammer Punch.

6. Elbow, Cutting Hand,Palm Strike,Double Cutting Hand.(used against 2 opponents)

7. Sweep Kick, Flat Back Kick, Double Cutting Hands.

8. Cutting Hand, Tiger Paw Punch, Cutting Hand.

9. Spear Fingers, Cutting Hand, Hammer Punch.

This set of nine moves like all the rest of the system is extreamly effective for defeating opponents when we have to fight to defend ourselves and our family and friends. It is also amazingly benificial for our health to train these moves on a daily basis. Like all the other aspects of the system the relaxed spiraling, twisting, rolling movements massage and heal the internal organs and invigourate the circulation of our internal energy.

Chapter 9
The Da Lu

The Da Lu , which translates as The Four Corners, is a continuous two person training method which teaches how to strike using continuous rebound energy. It also contains a special way of stepping which helps us defeat our opponents even when it seams as if they have the advantage. When they attack our arm instead of trying to pull it away from them, we use their pressure on our arm to step diagonally away from them and then to charge in and attack them with a diagonal shoulder strike.

Here is a simplified description of the Da lu.

A palm strikes **B** in the face (this is just to get the sequence started).

B vigorously tears **A**'s arm down and applies an elbow break and spear fingers to the throat.

A uses this momentum supplied by **B** to attack with shoulder strike and Spear Fingers.

B slips to the side and attacks **A** with Palm Strike to the jaw or Step Behind Bend Backwards to neck.

Now **A** and **B** do each others moves.

A vigorously tears **B**'s attacking forearm down and uses elbow break and spear fingers to throat.

B uses this momentum supplied by **A** to attack with shoulder strike and Spear Fingers.

B slips to the side and attacks **A** with Palm Strike to the jaw or Step Behind Bend Backwards to neck.

Now it swaps round again, the attacks and counters continue as the two training partners move in a clockwise direction around and around. The placement of the feet as they move around each other is the shape of a square. This is how the training method got its name because we are stepping to the four corners.

The Traditonal Chinese way of describing the movements of the main part of the Da Lu is to call them Tsai-Pull Down, Lieh-Split, Tsou-Elbow Strike and Kao-Shoulder Strike. These moves and the extra moves used for the direction change are all contained in the Pushing Hands System which is explained in the next chapter.

The extra movements of Double Palm Strike Cross Step or Forward Step Arm Twist can be added in to cause the direction of the Da Lu to change and become an anti clockwise stepping around the square. It can then change back again and again so we have a very vigorous continuous training method with an element of unpredictability because the direction change could happen at any time. It is on the change that a person unprepared for it becomes vulnerable. So we have to stay sensitive and aware and not just run through the movements.

As we release our fa jin energy in each strike the opponent rebounds of it and uses this for his counterattack. So like all of our taiji we are using fa jin and dim mak, as we rebound of the opponent. It is just that the rebound energy is more exaggerated and obvious in this particular exercise.

In all the two person contact training methods we are continuously rebounding of the opponents fa jin strikes. It is their fa jin energy which triggers us to fa jin them back which causes them to fa jin us again. Irrelevant of what strike the fa jin energy is used for, the fa jin energy is always the same. It is an exploding feeling caused by the incredibly vigorous shaking of the whole body, like when a dog has a rats head in its jaws and shakes its whole body violently to snap the rats neck.

The body moves like a spinning top on contact with another person, it is as if it was colliding with another spinning top, bouncing of it and then colliding again. This is the same principle whether we are training san sau or pushing hands or da lu. In all two person training methods there is a rebounding effect.

When we are practicing the single person forms by ourselves at the fa jin level then there is also a rebound sensation at the end of each move which causes us to fa jin shake into the next move and the process is repeated.

We release vast amounts of energy in each fa jin but we take some of that energy back into ourselves in the rebound for the next move so that we seem to be able to expend qi without losing qi. So that when we finish a form we feel that we have more energy than when we began. We are exhilarated but not exhausted and invigorated but not drained.

All the training methods are different but the principles that run through them all are the same so that at a very advanced level they all start to overlap and change into one another. It takes about twenty years to get to this level of understanding and ability but until one gets to this point it is not possible to appreciate the system as a whole.

Each of the separate parts of the Old Yang Style are outstanding but only when they have all been developed to a high level and can blend into one another can one say that they have really mastered the system. For example whilst blasting ones way through the advanced large san sau it might spontaneously happen that one finds oneself doing an attack and counterattack sequence from the advanced double pushing hands which then this flows effortlessly into part of the da lu and then ends with one of the twelve dim mak palms. Not as a prearranged idea but just as a subconscious reflex reaction.

So eventually you get to the stage of full contact fa jin, dim mak, free fighting with totally spontaneous moves that all flow together. It would be dangerous for beginners to try and attempt this level of training. It should only be attempted after the whole system has been learnt to a high level and then it should happen naturally.

We should remember that Chang yui chun trained full time from the age of fifteen to thirty five with Yang shao hu just to learn the system. He said that there were things contained in the forms and training methods that could not be taught but only understood after many years of ones own continuous dedicated training. The system itself revealed things to those who trained regularly all their lives.

Chapter 10
Single Pushing Hands and Double Pushing Hands

The whole of The Old Yang Style System is brought together in the Double Pushing Hands. Every conscious technique and every subconscious non technique, every type of attack and counter, every training method and principle that is in the system is within the two person Pushing Hands training methods. Single Pushing Hands and Double Pushing Hands should really be called Striking Hands rather than Pushing Hands because in The Old Yang Style there are only fa jin strikes. We have no pushing or pulling, no throws or grappling techniques, only strikes.

Yang Lu Chan created the single and double pushing hands from his knowledge of the Twelve Hand Weapons of Wu dang. Pushing hands gives us the sensitivity and integrated whole body movement that we need to not be where the opponent is attacking, whilst we attack him. And to know his intention without him knowing ours.

We learn how to acquire vast amounts of information about his speed, momentum, direction and weight distribution as well as his intention through the skin contact of pushing hands. It is as if we were listening to his thoughts and seeing his next intended attack before it occurs all through the skin contact. Chang yui chun described this phenomenon as 'Thinking with your skin'.

With single pushing hands we practice facing each other quite close together, at approximately the same distance that you would be if you were exchanging punches with an opponent. We are in a normal standing stance with the knees just unlocked, we have the feet positioned so that the back foot almost points straight ahead and the front toes are turned in slightly, this causes our internal structure to become very sturdy and robust. We have just one of our arms connected to theirs, by turning the hips from side to side a circular motion is created with the hands.

The hands actually passes through four different positions which blend into one another until there is just the appearance of a single circle.

The four positions are known as Ward Off (Peng in Chinese), Roll Back (Lu in Chinese), Press (Chee in Chinese) and Push (An in Chinese). Ward Off is when we strike with the back of the hand, Roll Back is a downwards turning strike, Press we usualy call Squeeze and is an attack with the back of the wrist and last of all Push which is a palm strike.

Pushing hands like every other part of the system is a training method, it is not a fight but it will give you abilities that can help you in a fight. In a fight you are always in opposition to the person who is attacking you but obviously when training there has to be an element of co operation with your training partner.

We put into our pushing hands all the qi gong in the internal power chapter and all the principles in the fa jin chapter and of course all the strikes that we practice are to dim mak points.

Single pushing hands gets the body to move in the correct way to strike with maximum fa jin power and also teaches us about how to move and where to move to in a fight to have the tactical advantage over the opponent. In pushing hands it is their attacking movement which moves us out of the line of their attack. It also positions us in the best place to be able to hit them.

So we never try and stop them from attacking us because it is to our advantage. If we did stop their attack they would then do another type of attack and we remain the victim. We subconsciously learn from the training of pushing hands that their attack activates our extreme yang energy and causes us to become the attacker and reply to the beginning of their attacking move with an even more offensive counter attack. In the pushing hands just like in a real combat situation as they come forwards we go forwards to hit them.

The way we train pushing hands and the attacks and counters is with very abstract movements, each one is a strike but not obviously so. The reason for this is that abstract movements go straight into the subconscious. So that what we have achieved in our training is a lightning fast fa jin subconscious reflex reaction. Later in the training the martial meaning of the movements is explained.

Many other martial arts styles will also say that after years of training their moves also become subconscious reflexes. The difference is that in all the other styles the moves are learnt as conscious techniques first and then they eventually go down into the subconscious. In the Old Yang Style we learn the moves subconsciously first and from there they can be released as a reflex reaction with out having to think about what to do.

With pushing hands the feet are continually shuffling because they are being moved by the waist/hip turn just as much as the hands are. We also learn to let our bodies be moved by the opponents attack into the correct counterattack position.

We begin with single attacks and counters, some are practised whilst still in front of the opponent others involve stepping around the opponent.

If the opponent attacks with a palm strike from the hand that is connected to ours it is countered with either an evasive body move created by a weight shift combined with a reshaping of the bodies posture or by an extra twist to position us on the outside of their lead hand. Our whole body is moving together as a single unit, we never just move the arm independently.

We also can counter by having the power of their attack cause us to make a change step and attack their face with our free hand. It is literally the power and force of their attack which created the momentum for our counter attack, almost as if it was them who made us hit them !

The opponent has a counter move to intercept our attack, he simply also does a change step and attacks our face with his free hand. These two back hand blows intercept each other before either of them land, it is the back of the attacking forearms which smash together.

The ideas contained in this little training method are repeated in many other parts of the system. The first aspect is that we experienced a heavy contact with another person, the contact was on a part of the body that will get sturdier from the contact and become an asset to us in a fight. Rather than the blow landing on the intended knock out points on the face which would end the training straight away.

So we can repeat the sequence again and again with both the right and left sides until we have learnt the ideas. Also we can learn to experience the body shock of hitting someone and being hit by them so that we can desensitise to it, so in a fight we can concentrate on defeating the opponent.

There are many variations of stepping with either foot as we strike with either hand. These are all practised separately and then after a degree of familiarity with each of the moves has been developed we can attack each other at random and always have a counter. So the movement is a spontaneous reflex reaction to an unknown random attack which always positions us so that we can counterattack with the greatest fa jin force to the weakest point on the opponent.

There is another similar small sequence in single pushing hands which involves attacks with Spear fingers, Hook Punches, Penetration punches and Uppercuts. These also begin as separate methods, then they are also all mixed up and trained in all possible combinations. It becomes apparent that whatever the attack is does not matter, our response is always the same type of body movement. We use the whole body to simultaneously evade forwards with a fa jin counterattack.

We also are able to train a wide variety of anti grabbing methods in our push hands, it does not matter which hand he uses to grab our wrist. He could grab one or both wrists our response is always the same, we never try and stop him applying the grab attack, we instead concentrate on using our whole body to simultaneously evade forwards with a fa jin counterattack to a dim mak point. We either hit him with the elbow of the grabbed hand or the with the spear fingers of the free hand.

It is important to remember that we never counter a grab with a grab, we strike. So when he is close enough to grab we are close enough to strike and should already have hit him.

The grab itself is only the weapon being used by the opponent against us and so it is not important, it is the person using the weapon that we need to defeat. So we attack their neck, throat, eyes and skull and as a side effect they loose their ability to use the grab.

In taiji we use the same idea when the opponent has a knife or a stick or a brick, all these items are harmless in themselves. It is the person who is holding them that is dangerous, so we never block the weapon. And we never try and grab the hand holding the weapon because he would just hit us with the other hand. We never try and disarm the attacker because he would then either rearm or attack again with his fists, feet (and knees, elbows and head !).

What we always do is evade the weapon whilst moving forwards and attack their neck, throat, eyes and skull with fa jin and dim mak. Then because they are knocked out or dead on the ground whether they attacked us with a weapon or used their fist as a weapon is irrelevant.

With double pushing hands we incorporate everything that I have already mentioned for single pushing hands and we have both forearms in contact with theirs. By turning the hips from side to side a rolling motion is created with the hands, they can go either clockwise or anti clockwise. The hands pass through four different positions which blend into one another until there is just a continuous rolling motion.

The four positions in double pushing hands are known by the same names as in single pushing hands but they actualy are more complicated because now obviously both hands are involved. Ward Off is when we strike with the back of the hand and the other arm is in a low Ward Off position which we call the Hinge Arm, Roll Back is a downwards turning strike now with both hands not just one, Press we usualy call Squeeze and is an attack with the back of the wrist this time the rear hand supports the lead hand wrist strike and last of all Push which is now a double palm strike.

Whenever we use double palm strike we always have one hand yin and the other yang. We never have them both equal because then there would not be a strong enough energy flow either for healing or for fighting.

In double pushing hands we also use the movements known as Tsai-Pull Down, Lieh-Split, Tsou-Elbow Strike and Kao-Shoulder Strike which we learnt in our training of the Da Lu excersise.

These eight moves Ward Off, Roll Back, Press and Push, Pull Down, Split, Elbow and Shoulder Strike are not just specific techniques but are also ways of moving. So that we could do a diffrent move from another part of The Old Yang Style System but it would be based on one of these eight ways of doing things.

Before we put in any of the fighting principles that we have within our double pushing hands and before we practice the attacks and counters we must first get the way of moving working correctly, this could be thought of as a neutral state. We need to get a continuose regular flow without any uncomfortable or unbalanced movements. Once this neutral state has been gained then we can practice adding in the internal qi gong, the fa jin and the various details about the up and down left and right back and forwards aspects of the way of moving plus the various types of yin and yang pressures and sensations.

There are two attacking forwards pressures, a yin water and a yang fire pressure. The yang way of moving is with a very dense forceful overt power, like an explosion or a sledge hammer, this works but it is possible for the opponent to detect it because he can sense my yang intention. So once this type has been learnt we then train the way of attacking forwards with just as much density and force but we use a yin pressure which is covert, so the opponent only has a sensation of his contact with us but not our contact with him.

This way he is unable to pick up our intention and he has been hit before he knew he was being attacked. With this type of yin pressure the opponent feels like he is being drowned or suffocated by the gentle crushing effect of the coils of a boa constrictor.

If we are not practicing attacks and counters but are just going round and round with our double pushing hands then beginners should both be using a reasonable amount of yang fire force on each other to toughen themselves up and get used to heavy pressure. At an intermeadiate level one person should practice absorbing and desolving yang fire force with the yin water method. At an advanced level both practitioners are fire and water at the same time and can vary the degrees of each depending on the situation.

There are also two similar but diffrent types of pressure from the opponent that we need to develop our ability to detect. The first is a yang pressure, this is when just before a strike he puts more pressure onto your forearm because he intends to move through it as he attacks you. This type of pressure is quite easy to feel and respond to because it is a pressure increase. A yin pressure is very hard to sense because it is a reduction in pressure as he disconnects your forearm as he is moving to strike you.

When we have an awarness of both these types of pressure then we can increase our sensitivity to them. Once this is accomplished then we are able to have a response to his impending attack because we know it is on the way. To begin with our response time will be a few seconds then as the years go by our response time reduces untill it is simultainiouse with the opponents attack.

There is a higher level that is obtainable but it takes many, many years of reguler daily training to get there. It is eventualy possible to have your physical response prior to their physical attack. The way that this becomes possible is not illogical or nor does it go against the idea of cause and then effect. What is actualy happening when he attacks is that first he has the idea to attack, this is his mind moving, this will cause his energy to move and last of all his body will move.

So a begginer will only have the ability to detect his body moving and then respond with their counterattack, so the counter will be after attack. An intermeadiat level practitioner will be able to feel his energy move before his body and so the counterattack will be at the same time as the attack. An advanced level practitioner will be able to sense his mind move before his energy or his body and so the counterattack will reach the opponent before his attack has physically begun.

The various attacks are mostly executed from forty five degrees to the side. As he moves towards you, you angle to the side or as you move to him you angle to the side, or both of these at the same time. So we are able to move forwards and to the side as they move forwards towards us, so we have an attacking forwards way of moving the body as a counter attack to their attack. This is repeated continuously as we go around and around with the flowing movements of double pushing hands.

There are some attacks that are used head on but the way that we move is with a fa jin shake. So in fact we are attacking like a hammer drill, the hand is moving side to side and spiralling in a corkscrew shape as it strikes forwards with a hammer drilling effect. This movement is usually a Spear fingers strike to the throat or eyes.

It is very important that we never unnecessarily apply any pressure for no reason because he will then feel it and respond to it with an attack, so we have contact but only enough to read their intention, not enough to enable them to read ours.

All the attacks and counters that we practice are only slight variations on the way we are already moving our body. So when it appears to others that we are just going around and around we are also subconsciously practising the attacks and counters, Yang pan hou called this 'The idea always being there for attack'. His quotes on pushing hands really do communicate the essence of the art, 'look for your opponents weaknesses.....surprise attack the opponent with fa jin.....attack from the side.....evade and attack simultaneously......when in close strike with the shoulder, elbow and knee......always follow up a successful action without delay to finish the confrontation.'

The circular movement of the qi in the lower dan dien moves the hips and waist and belly in a circular way which moves the hands and feet in a circular way. So we naturally begin circling around each other whilst practising the movements of double pushing hands. The hands can go both clockwise and anti clockwise so equal to this our circling of the opponent will be clockwise or anti clockwise.

As well as this type of evasive manoeuvring we also have V stepping forwards with either leg irrelevant of whichever way the arms are circling. Once all these concepts have been trained for a sufficient amount of time we then practice a simple method of direction changing as a response to an attack. We cover both his hands with one of ours whilst the free hand attacks with a Side Palm Strike to his jaw. This causes the opponent to respond with a direction change as his counter to our attack. His counter contains an elbow strike to the temple which we do not physically connect with although in our minds we see it landing on the correct dim mak point.

So we are now at the stage where we can go in either direction and change direction and step forwards to attack and all the time as we flow through the moves and change direction we are moving the way we would where we to actually be applying the fa jin strikes. The next part of the training involves applying a single blow to the opponent at certain specific points in the rolling motion of the double pushing hands. For example if we imagine that the rolling movement of the hands is like the hands of a clock turning then at diffrent times on the clock face certain attacks are easier to achieve.

Each type of strike is designed to access a specific dim mak point and to make hitting these point a subconscious reflex based on feeling our position in relation to them rather than actually having to look for the points. Obviously in a fight there is no time to look, there is only a brief moment for your subconscious to work for you, in the most effective way, using what it has gained from the training of double pushing hands.

So the double pushing hands has little fa jin shuddering shakes within it and these become the single strikes that we train. Obviously we practice them slowly first to get the feeling for the correct timing distance and position. Then when we have the correct sensitivity and awareness and the ability to know their intention and hide our intention we start to practice these strikes as fa jin.

There are interwoven within the fa jin striking moves various ways of opening up the opponents defences. We can enter onto the inside or outside of their front or rear hand, cover both their hands with one or both of our hands. Also we have the Yang way of violently smash aside their arms as we move in and the Yin way of slipping past their defences so that they do not know anything is happening untill it is to late and they have already been hit.

Everything that we do is dependant on our sensitivity more than anything else. A person may have fa jin and dim mak but these skills will not be effective unless we have the sensitivity to feel when, where and how to use them.

Here is a list of some of the basic single strikes that we first practice.

Hammer Hand strike into his jaw.
Heal Palm strike into his temple.
Tiger Paw Punch up into the eye or throat.
Back Hand into his eye socket .
Open Back Palm to neck.
Heel Palm up under chin.
Horizontal Slashing Fingers across eyes.
Spear Fingers Strike into his throat.
Cobra Strike into his eyes. .
Upside down and Reverse Cobra Strike into his eyes.
Horizontal and Vertical and Reverse Elbow to neck, throat and temple.
Forwards and Reverse Shoulder Strike into his heart.
Rising Cupped palm Strike into his jaw.
Horizontal Cupped Calm strike to side of neck.
Curving Back Cupped palm strike into his spine or skull.
Falling Heel Palm strike into his floating rib.
Hidden Hand Punch into his floating rib.
Descending Spiral Hammer into his kidney.
Rising Curve Penetration Punch into skull.
Descending Curve Penetration Punch into neck, outside and inside.
Reverse Hand Penetration Punch into neck.

Once these single strikes have been learnt we then practice applying two strikes from the same hand on one fa jin movement to two different dim mak points, here are some examples.

Hammer Hand strike into his jaw then the same hand
strikes with a Heel Palm into his temple.

Cobra strike into his eyes then the same hand
strikes with a Tiger Paw up into one of his eyes.

Flat Back Palm strike over his eye socket then the same hand
strikes with Spear Fingers to his throat.

Finger Blade slash to eye then the same hand
strikes with Reverse Finger Blade slash to the other eye.

Spear Fingers to his neck then the same hand
strikes with the Hook Hand to the neck and jaw.

Elbow strike him in skull and then the same hand
strikes with Knife Edge Hand into the face.

Once these have been learnt we then practice using both hands for multiple attacks, here are some examples.

Rising Hammer Hand Punches up into temple then
leg sweep and Forearm Bar their neck.

Falling Hammer Hand Punch down into kidneys then
Forearm Bar their neck and Palm Strike temple.

Heel Palm down into kidneys then Elbow Strike into neck.

Palm Strike into neck then Elbow Strike to neck then
Heal Palm Strike to back of head.

Palm Strike into his solar plexus then Rising Elbow neck
then Knife Hand neck and jaw.

Double Heel Palms to neck then leg sweep, knee to groin
and cobra fingers to eyes.

Three Tigerpaw Punches to ribs then Rising Diagonal Elbow to heart.

Cutting Fingers to eyes then attack central nervouse sysytem
then Tiger claws eyes and Side Palm jaw.

Three Cutting Fingers to eyes and Double Cutting Fingers to neck
then Elbow Strike to neck.

Elbow strike to kidneys then Elbow Strike to solar plexus
then Palm Strikes to kidney and head.

We then practice attacks and counters, these flow back into the rolling movement of the double pushing hands. Here are a few examples of some attacks and counters.

Arm Break with Spear fingers to neck
is countered by Elbow Strike to throat.

Arm Break with Spear fingers to neck
is countered by Reverse Shoulder Strike to the heart.

Falling spiral Punch to the liver
is countered by Heel Palm Strike to the back of the head.

Open back palm to face
is countered by Elbow Strike to the neck.

Forearm to the heart
is countered by Back Palm to jaw.

Elbow Strike to the neck
is countered by Elbow Strike to the solar plexus.

Double Heel palm Strikes to liver and spleen
are countered by Double Hook hand to neck.

Shoulder Strike to the heart
is countered by Elbow Strike to the solar plexus.

Elbow Strike to the neck
is countered by Spear Fingers to the eyes.

Penetration punch to the neck
is countered by Heel Palm Strike to the temple.

Spear Fingers to the throat is countered by Arm Break .

When the practitioners are more accomplished there are also responses to the counters and like most other aspects of the Old Yang Style it then becomes full contact free fighting.

In all our pushing hands training we are learning some very subtle things to do with our awareness, that are necessary to know about for it to be effective. If these subtle things are not understood then no matter how many attacks and counters one knows, non of them will work.

The first thing is not to telegraph to the opponent that you are going to attack. So just before you attack don't alter your speed or tense or let your intention show on your face. Also don't let the qi in the skin that has contact with them increase gradually as you build up to a strike, just go from normal to full power with out any indicators for them to read.

We are practising concealing our intention whilst becoming more sensitive to the opponents. Just attack in the moment with out revealing your intention, have an empty mind (wuji), don't think about when you are going to attack or when you think he is going to attack. Just enter into the wuji state of being and act spontaneously in the moment with your attack or with a reflex action with your counter attack.

It is also important to remember that just going round and round with the double pushing hands movements with a training partner, not obviously doing the attacks and counters is incredibly beneficial. Our subconscious is continually imagining the attacks and counters so even when it seams as if we are not practicing the applications, deep down inside we are. Also all the great healing benefits of the old yang style that have been mentioned elsewhere in this book are all present in the double pushing hands.

For serious practitioners of this art, as well as training all the forms and two person training methods one should also be practising the double pushing hands every day. Our body is like a spring the pressure of our training partner on us compresses that spring and gives us potential energy. We then release this into them which compresses them and so it goes on and on. If a spring is left alone it rusts, only through regular compression and release will it maintain its vibrancy and power. It is the same with the body, only regular daily training can enable us to maintain our health and internal power, keep ourselves strong, improve our resistance to disease and increase our chances of having a long happy and healthy life.

Chapter 11
Fighting

Before we get into fighting we need to first cover not fighting. The first most important thing is don't be where fights happen, avoid known trouble spots. Any place, a club, bar or part of town which has a reputation for violence should be avoided. Second all the people who are known to be aggressive or who look like they are looking for trouble should be avoided.

Be steady within yourself, don't attract attention by inappropriate displays of wealth or with confrontational egotistic behaviour. Don't make eye contact with an aggressor, this will just provoke him to have a go. Of course don't live like a mouse but also don't make yourself a target. Avoid trouble by not being in unnecessary conflict with others. If you stick to the above points you win by not fighting.

Always carry with you a second wallet with some cash in it, so if a mugger pulls out a knife and demands your money you can give him that. He's got what he wanted and you still have most of your cash, your credit cards and most importantly your good health and life.

Not fighting at all, is top of the list, the best victory ever. If it is possible engage the opponent in conversation try and diffuse the situation, if they are in a hightend state of aggitation then try and talk them down to normality.

If a fight is unavoidable then having trained The Old Yang Style of Taiji will help you to win. The Old Yang Style is the culmination of generations of development by people who devoted their whole lives to creating a martial art to defeat opponents. It was realised that a martial art that concentrated on self defence would not ensure success, only by concentrating on the opponents defeat could survival in a fight be assured.

All our movements are naturally occurring movements nothing is forced or complicated everything that we do is simple and based upon normal reflex actions. The opponent attacks in some way and our hands come up and forwards as our body uses the fa jin to explode forwards in to the attacker.

There are six types of responses we could have to an attack.

1.

We could just block his punches and kicks, if we did this then we would get worn down and he would eventually get through. So we never just block.

2.

We could block and then as our next move we could do a counter attack, if we did this we would loose because in the space between our block and counter he would have got another strike in and he would follow up his advantage. So we never block then strike.

3.

We could block and simultaneously counter attack in a very heavy handed yang way, this is going to get us closer to winning and is a good option to train but is still not the best option. We often use this method, it is effective and builds up our confidence. The small san sau fighting form has this type of emphasis to it.

4.

If we don't block in a heavy handed yang way but intercept in a yin deflecting way and move in with our block becoming the strike from a position where we cannot be hit but can hit them then we are really at an excellent level of ability and are very likely to win. This method we use a lot, it is trained mostly in the double pushing hands attacks and counters.

5.

An even more elegant way is to be so yin with the intercept that they have no information about our intentions. We have just a slight sensitive touch with them as we move to a position beside them. Or even better, there is no contact at all with their attack so that we can use all our energy and strength not on blocking their attack but on attacking them.

6.

The very best way of fighting is of course the pre emptive strike. In the taiji classics it says 'if he moves, we move first'. This can be explained on two different levels, first it means that if he goes to hit us we move with fa jin explosive power and get our strike to hit him first. On a deeper level it means that when we relax and sink our qi into our dan dien and into the ground our awareness expands out wards along with our depth of feeling in our periphery vision. We then have the ability to sense when their mind moves and we hit them first.

Their intention to hit us is actually the beginning of their attack, to actually wait for this to manifest as a physical movement is a waste of an opportunity. An observer may think that you hit the opponent first but you and the opponent both know the truth.

Chang yui chun developed eight preemptive attacking sequences to train a person in the correct timing distance and movement necessary to make the strikes work. Erle montaigue added one further excellent method. What is amazing about these nine ways are that they can be used against multiple attackers. To win when being attacked by two or three people is a lot easier if you attack first. You can go for the leader or the biggest person first to weaken the confidence of the others. Or more usually you just begin by attacking the person who is closest to you.

This first strike idea has so many benefits that if it can be achieved then you are going to win before the fight begins. This is the perfect move but it relies on a level of awareness about the developing situation.

There are certain indicators that the opponent is getting ready to attack, his face starts to go red, he makes threats and swears, puffs up his chest and starts to make aggressive gestures with his hands. These are prefight tactics to try and get you to back down or to try and steal your energy.

Whichever way you respond there are six things you must always maintain, keep your centre of gravity low and your energy flowing and your breathing centred and have it as your intention to hit the opponent hard and fast repeatedly, whether you do or not you must be geared up for it should you need to, keep your hands up and away from you towards him and last of all hide your intention from him.

So because the fight is not yet on you could decide to try and talk him down to a more reasonable level, being firm and clear, if necessary apologise if you think it will help diffuse the situation. Or you could be very yang and intimidate him with even more overt displays of aggressive behaviour if you think you can get him to back down. Or if it is possible you could leave whilst staying in a controlled and aware state of mind. If the opponent is threatening to attack you but has not actualy begun his attack and states that what he wants is to steal your wallet or bag etc then give him your belongings and avoid a fight. Avoiding unnessecary physical injury is always the best option.

However if he has already begun his attack by rushing towards you then you can hit him first, or if you think he is reaching for a knife concealed in his clothes then don't hesitate strike pre emptivly. Never telegraph your intention to hit him preemptively, go from normal to berserk without any pre fight indicators that could alert him to your intention. This is what is ment by the statement from the taiji classics which says, 'know yourself, know others but remain unknown'.

We make sure that we don't let him see us position ourselves so we are standing in the best place to hit him. Also if you see that he is shifting his position to be in a good position to hit you, as soon as he starts to do this, don't wait, hit him first.

So if you choose to be extremely yang then be the most aggressive abusive confrontational 'mad staring eyes' lunatic he has ever encountered with your hand gesturing in the air in front of his face (doing qi disruption techniques) and whilst you have got his mind engaged in your diversionary antics you have covered the ground to get close enough to him to hit him first.

After you have hit him, hit him again and again till he is down and out. (Of course you used Taiji - fa jin - dim mak - continuous attacks). So you never had to fight him, it was not an exchange of blows, it was not a fair fight, he declared war so you launched a covert pre emptive strike.

This is extreme I know but if there was a second attacker you would not want to be involved in an unneccerally long exchange of blows with the first. You would want to finish the first opponent as quickly as possible to be able to concentrate on the second. So this way of the pre emptive attack means you have destroyed the first opponent, without having taken any unnecessary injuries yourself and if there is a second assailant you are in better shape to fight him and are again going to be fighting only one person. (I hear you say what if there are three of them, well then assume you are going to die and with your last breath on this planet dedicate your life to taking as many of them with you as you can).

Alternatively you could choose to be very yin, when he challenges you, walk towards him as you lift your hands up (palms towards him) and as you are saying 'Look I'm sorry I really don't want any kind of trouble' suddenly hit him. The words are purely to get him to lower his guard both physically and mentally and this combined with the 'hands up' posture enables you cover the distance, engaged his mind, whilst you are readying your body, so that you can then hit him first, from close range, with great force repeatedly until he is down and out.

Again we are not fighting according to any rules or regulations nor are we trying to see who is faster or stronger, all we are doing is winning the fight. Many people who train in the martial arts are not comfortable with this way of doing things. However we have to realise that there is a difference between martial arts training and fighting.

When we are training it is a warm blooded situation with people who we know and there is a certain amount of respect and organised conduct. In a fight it is against a stranger, it is cold blooded and there is nothing arranged, it is an ugly situation that should be avoided.

It is very very important to hit him first because in the majority of fights whoever hits first wins. For those of you who are thinking that this is a bit extreme, remember the type of person you are dealing with is a madman, this is someone who wants to harm you, to want to fight is a type of madness.

These kind of people need help to work through their unresolved mental issues and emotional imbalances and become more sensible people. However before you can help these people to heal themselves of their madness, your first concern is staying alive through the next five minuets !!!

So save your concern for them for later and concentrate yourself on the necessary task ahead, to win at all costs. The training of taiji as a martial art is not competitive, we work with our training partners to help them improve their ability, not to get one up on them. However fighting is not training it is a competition but one in which there is no second place, no silver medal for a good effort. There is just one winner and the looser gets hit and goes down. I read in the papers on a regular basis of people who are kicked to death once they are on the ground. Do not go to the ground, stand and fight, fight and win, win every time.

There are some other pre fight indicators which are more serious than the ones mentioned earlier. If the opponents face goes pale, their voice becomes monotone and slower and they stop their movements and go still then they are just about to explode with violence. They may ready themselves with a lowering of the head, a positioning of the feet and the shoulders shifting as the hands begin to clench and they either have eyes that cloud over or glance at available targets on your body.

They might also try a trick or two like indicating that they are going to turn and walk away or look away to make you think they are going to leave but this is just a set up to distract you. If any of these things happen then they have decided to hit you and any chance of talking them down or distracting them has gone, just hit them, don't wait, hit them hard and fast.

We of course use these two set ups mentioned above on our opponents to distract them. We also have other ways of diverting their attention for example like lifting our hand up so they follow its movement for a split second and whilst they are looking up we kick low to their knee with Chang yui chun's No. 7 Pre emptive attack.

We can also look at the situation from another perspective which is where they are in relation to you. If they are blocking the only exit it means that they are not going to give you the option of escape and want to fight in which case hit them first. If they are staying outside your kicking range it means that they are not committed to attacking you and are not convinced they will win. In this case you have a greater chance of being able to talk the situation down and avoid a fight.

If they are about to step into your space then this means that they are confident and are trying to cover the distance to be close enough to strike. They may talk or shout to distract you or wave their hands, don't be distracted by this, the important thing to notice is that they are stepping forwards into your space, this is the beginning of their attack. Whether they have begun to throw their punch or not does not matter, it is their forwards movement which is the attacking movement we have to counter. So don't wait for their punch, hit them, hit them hard and fast and follow it up till they are down and out.

This idea is expressed very clearly in the classics of taiji, it says 'If they go back you go back, if they move forwards you move forwards'. So it is all about understanding timing and distance, if they go back and you go forwards, you will walk onto their strike. So what we do is when they go back we go back so there is no fight.

If they move forwards to attack you and you go back they will keep on attacking because your retreat will reinforce the idea in their minds that they are the aggressor and you the victim. So we turn it all around and as they move forwards we move forwards, we become the predator and make them the prey.

They expected us to freeze on the spot or retreat, instead we do the unexpected, we advance. This way we win the mind game and also are positioning ourselves in a better place to win the physical fight. By attacking them before they strike or as they are beginning to move we are turning the mind game around. Even if they have got half way into their first punch we still attack forwards this makes us the aggressor and reinforces our yang energy, it makes us more powerful in mind and body and unsettles them.

They will have two shocks the first will be a very heavy physical strike to one of their dim mak points delivered with fa jin the second will be the realisation that they are not facing a weaker human target but an enraged tiger.

There is now a moment when their mind and body is trying to adapt and cope with the fact that instead of hitting they are being hit and instead of being the hammer they are now the anvil. It is in this moment that we continue to release our fa jin dim mak strikes each one causing more damage than the last never giving them the chance to regain their momentum. We ruthlessly press the advantage striking repeatedly to the neck, throat, eyes and head. We complete the shaking fa jin attack with a devastating finishing movement for example a forearm slam across the throat as we claw their eyes and drag their head backwards and down twisting their neck as our rising knee slams them in the back of the head.

This is a bit extreme but we are not competing for medals we are fighting for our lives, what if he had a concealed knife, what if there was more than one attacker? we cannot spend a long time dancing with the first opponent we have to cut them down like lightning to be ready for a second assailant. Our strike must be like an axe chopping, like a sword cutting and like a spear stabbing. We must make our whole body the weapon and strike with the nearest part of our body to the nearest part of theirs.

For example we kick and punch with the front foot and hand, this way they have less warning of our attack. We are able to generate massive force for these blows because we are using fa jin, without the power of fa jin a lead leg or lead hand attack might not be enough to stop them. When we attack there is no drawing back to get ready this would alert them to our intention. We just explode forwards with continuous fa jin dim mak strikes, if they are throwing a punch we hit their arm and rebound of it into an attack to their neck or head.

When we leap forwards it is off our front leg that we have our weight on. If we shifted our weight back on to our rear leg, to make it easier to lift our front leg of the ground to step forwards. Then we would have wasted a move that we could have used for hitting the opponent and also of course we are wasting time which could cost us our lives.

Our fighting stance to the untrained observer just looks like a normal standing stance but we have some slightly different arrangements within our body so that we are ready for anything. Our back foot points almost straight ahead and front foot has the toes turned in slightly to creates a very strong internal structure for us to transfer power from the ground through us and also by having the front foot turned in a bit it means our knee will be protecting our groin from a kick. We have the 'C' shaped back like a mountain gorilla just before it attacks and we use the taiji classic saying of 'look left gaze right and look right gaze left'.

This means that the direction our eyes are pointing and the direction our mind is looking are opposite. So he thinks we are not looking at him but we are, this way he is not prompted to attack because we have not challenged him with our eye contact but if he moves we know it and we hit him as a subconscious reflex action. This is because the periphery view connects directly to the subconscious mind.

So if they enter our personal space we hit them, if they are thinking about attacking us we hit them, if they actually begin the first five percent of their punch or kick we hit them. The idea is we have the initiative, we don't ever wait until their blow is just about to land on us before we respond and if we are only reacting after we have been hit then obviously we need to train more often for longer to increase our reflex action response speed.

If we are ever forced by their attack to step back then even as we are going back we are striking forwards. As we move we turn and release a devastating penetration punch which will be doubly effective because they are walking on to it or we kick them between the legs. Whatever we do it reflects the fact that even if we are appearing to step back we are still on the offensive with the intention of defeating the opponent. In the worst case when you have already been hit they expect you to be stunned so they can follow up their strike but we always do the unexpected. We have a built in reflex from our training that causes us to respond by going as mad as a rabid dog with an instant explosion of berserka counter attacking dim mak fa jin strikes whenever we are hit.

If there are no indicators that a fight is about to begin and you are just suddenly attacked with no warning then because of the dedicated years of training in the old yang style we have the taiji reflex action response. We simultaneously counterattack using our automatic reflex training which causes us to V step and use fa jin - dim mak - continuous attacks, repeatedly striking the opponents eyes, neck and throat etc.

Remember its not a competition for points with a referee saying what is and is not allowed, there are no rounds and you can't tap out or rely on help arriving, its about winning to stay alive, you have to be ruthless to survive. You have to put honour and fair play to one side and win. A fight is not decided on points, nor is it decided by who is the last man standing, it is decided by who is the last one still moving.

Remember that the crimminal who is about to attack you is relying on you bieng unaware or confused so stay clear minded and aware. If a stranger comes up to you and asks the time don't look down at your watch because this is when he will attack you. Instead lift your hands up between you and the opponent create a distance look at your watch when it is up so you can keep your head up. Let him know that you are onto him and you are ready, this way he may not try and rob you but go off and look for a person who is less aware and more vulnerable.

Another example might be if a stranger comes up to you and asks you for directions , don't turn away from him and point the way, instead lift your hands up between you and the opponent and create a distance. Look at him and see if you are bieng set up, if you think you are then say you think it is that way and point in the direction behind him away from you.

Don't carry a bag if you can help it, put things in your pockets, if you find yourself in the wrong part of town put your jewlery in your pocket. Avoid the attention of oppertunistic crimminals. Stay aware and clear minded, be calm and steady within yourself and always whilst hoping for the best be prepared for the worst.

All the information in this book about how to defeat an attacker is just as much for women as for men. Both men and women need to know that they have the animal potential within themselves to be very aggressive and determined. If the attacker is a man or a woman or if the person being attacked is a man or a woman the same principles still apply. You must be outraged that you have been targeted and respond with unexpected ferocious force.

For you to be successful you must always have a strategy that is based on what the taiji classics say. We have already discussed the meaning of 'If he moves, we move first' and 'If they go back you go back, if they move forwards you move forwards'. The one which needs more explanation because it is of such great relevance to fighting is 'Know yourself and know others but remain unknown'.

This relates to the strategy we use in a fight and the way we fight, some examples of strategy, if a loonatic for no reason pics on you and challenges you to a fight and he will not accept your appoligies and excuses but says "You and me, outside now" then as you both leave the club-pub-bar if he is in front of you then hit him from behind. If you are in front of him then as he steps through the door behind you, slam it closed into his face and then follow through with fa jin dim mak attacks.

If a mad man wants to beat you up to prove he is a better fighter and refuses to listen when you tell him that he is the better fighter. Then when he makes his final statment something like 'right put em up' or 'Ok you and me fair fight' the first thing you should do is hit him before he finishes the sentence.

If the opponent says that he is going to 'beat you into a pulp' or 'make you regret you were ever born' or any other extream declaration of his intentions and then he goes to take his jacket off. Don't wait for him to get ready, when his jacket is half off and he is temporarily restricted in his movement, punch him repeatedly in the head neck and throat.

The important thing to remember is that the opponent might actualy be a better fighter with more experience so don't fight him defeat him before the fight begins.

If you are about to be attacked by a man getting out of his car, if you can then run to safety if it is close, if not then don't run away from him because he will get back in his car and run you down. Instead run towards him and as he is getting out the car kick the door closed onto his hands, feet and head.

If you are in a foreign country and you are in an argument and are challenged to a fight then agree a time and a place to sort it out and don't turn up, fly home. Always do the unexpected without indicating your intentions.

If you have not been able to avoid a fight and it has begun and they throw a punch and we intercept it, we could change our intercept into a counter or we could be doing a simultaneous counter with the other hand. The initial intercept is what we need to know about to make use of 'Know yourself and know others but remain unknown'.

As we connect with them we are receiving vast amounts of information through the skin contact about his direction of force and his intention. We learn to read these things through our two person contact training like pushing hands and san sau. He also is trying to get information about us from this contact, so he is expecting to hit us in the face or for us to hammer his arm and stop his punch. Which ever of these two signals he gets lets him know that he should now attack with a punch from the other hand.

So what we do is to have our intercept as a type of guide to draw his hand along the line of flight it was originally on whilst we move out of the way of his fist. We don't move his arm away, we move around his arm. So he has not felt a block or a contact with us so he will carry on with his punch assuming he is winning and just about to smash us in the face and not know that it has failed and he should be throwing the other punch. It is in this moment of extra time that we have acquired for ourselves that we hit him with fa jin dim mak repeatedly and relentlessly until he is defeated. So we know what we are doing and know what he is doing but he is unaware of our subtle strategy.

The above method makes him think he is winning as we are setting up his defeat, there are many other things we can make him think as we contact on the intercept. We can transmit subconsciously to the opponent various messages, we can get him to lose his desire to attack, we can also contact in such a way that his attention is drawn to his arm. So whilst his mind is temporarily distracted we can hit him. Also we can bring his energy from his body into his arm so it is temporarily depleted in his body so our fa jin dim mak strikes to his torso and head will be even more devastating because his defensive energy has been taken away from these areas. All these subtle methods are taught within the Old Yang Style system and are what is ment by the taji classic saying of 'Know yourself and know others but remain unknown'.

There is another quote from the classics which explains in even more detail the timing and movement we should have in a fight, 'Lead his strength to nothing, then attack immediately, adhere, stick, and follow him without losing him'. This means when he throws his first punch he expects you to be hit, or to block or evade and then counter with your punch. Basically his preconception of the fight is based around the idea of, my go - your go, my go - your go. So what we do is attack as he is beginning his first punch either physically or if you are well trained enough when he is starting to think about punching. So what is happening is he is beginning with 'my go' and before he has really even got this far we are having our go. So as soon as he moves his body (or if you are sensitive enough as soon as he moves his mind) you are going, my go, my go, my go, my go, my go etc

So he goes to punch us in the face and we let the movement of his body move us into a position to not be hit by him but be in the best position to hit him. Whilst we are letting this happen he has the feeling of being just about to hit our face but never quite reaching the target because we are no longer in the place where he was aiming for. This is 'Lead his strength to nothing'.

So now that we have moved forwards and slightly to the side by sort of walking around him we can hit him with fa jin. We begin our movement around him with one big slap step at about forty five degrees to our right or left this will put us at forty five degrees to his centre. It is from here that we have our first fa jin strike, this is the meaning of 'then attack immediately'.

The fa jin rebound of our first strike causes us to shuffle step a bit further around him as we strike again. This action is repeated again and again so we end up standing behind him having hit him continuously on dim mak points as we moved around his body. The hand that was not hitting him was controlling his body and closest arm. This is 'Adhere, stick, and follow him without losing him'.

The first strikes he would have received would be on his centreline on the front of his body, eyes, throat, solar plexus and groin. As we moved around his body to the side we would be striking to his temple, the side of his neck and the side of his rib cage. And once we have got behind him we would be striking to the back of his head, his kidneys and his spine.

We always protect our centreline, this is the line from the nose down to the navel. On this line are many vulnerable targets that we don't want to get hit, eyes, throat, solar plexus, lower dan dien access point and of course the groin. Also of course we have these as some of our primary targets when striking the opponents body. We have our hands up in front forming a triangle shape so his attacks are deflected to the outside of our arms away from our centre line. We are then able to cut in to his centre line and attack him.

There is another centre line which is an imaginary line from the middle top of his head (acupuncture point Governing meridian 20) straight down to his perineum (acupuncture point Conception meridian1). The way to imagine this is that the inside edges of the segments of an orange all lead to the centre of the orange.

It makes no difference were on the surface of the orange you hit you can always aim it towards the centre. The reason we do this is because if we aimed slightly of centre then like an orange the opponent would be able to rotate and some of the force would be deflected. However if we aim into his centre all our fa jin power goes into him and he cannot dissipate the shockwave. Even if we do not land our blows on to dim mak points but just fa jin into his centreline we can cause him extreme internal damage and he will collapse. We of course are always rotating to deflect his attacks away from our centerline so that the energy of his strike is dispersed.

When fighting an opponent we are always ever so slightly sideways on. This means that the side of ours that is closest to them will have the elbow of our lead hand over the knee of our lead leg and the rear hand will be over our centre line (from our nose to our navel). If we turn then the arms also change so that this principle always remains the same. Of course all these principles are contained within all the forms that we train so that they become subconscious and are always there for us when we need them.

I have talked a lot about what to do as if taiji had very specific techniques for each type of attack, we do train a lot of movements in our taiji but non of them are techniques. We do make the taiji movements into a wide variety of techniques but they are not fixed nor are there a limited number of uses for each move. Everything that we do is about a way of moving and a way of being. When we combine these together we have a way of fighting.

If some one attacked me with a very specific move like a straight left punch to my head I do not know what my counter attack would be. My hands would go up and out towards him and intercept his arm, then on contact, depending on his direction of movement and my movement and how the pressure of his attack moves me I would end up in a certain position. What this position is I have no way of knowing in advance. I might be on the inside or the outside of his arm, I might be now standing in front of him to the one side or behind him. I would then hit any dim mak points that I had access to, which ones they ended up being I have no way of knowing in advance.

All of the above takes place in an instant, my response is all an instinctive reaction that taiji has helped cultivate but what I do is not a specific taiji move from one of the taiji forms or two person training methods. All our taiji training is designed to awaken within us our own fighting ability, to bring out the instinctive survival mechanism that is hidden within us all. It has many different names, the reptile mind or the animal within or seeing the red mist. Whatever we call it is not so important, the essential thing is that when you are in that moment you are able to explode into an uncontrollable rage and tear your opponent apart like a lion among sheep.

Within the Old Yang Style of Taiji we have special internal triggers that we are taught to activate within certain training methods. The use of these triggers helps us to tap into our reptile minds and release the animal within, this gives us the extreme yang qi power for the explosive fa jin movement that we need to destroy all in our path and prevail even under the most adverse of conditions.

We have mad eyes which are glaring and staring like a lunatic, our ears pull back against our skull and we are shouting like a lion roaring. Our fingers are extended like claws and our back is up like a cornered cat, even our hair is standing up on our heads we are so full of yang qi. All these animalistic things trigger our wild side and give us the bezerk aggression we need to smash and crush the opponent. This is how a small person can defeat an apparently bigger and stronger person.

Looked at from the other perspective if we are observing a person who is mentally deranged and has gone berserk he will be displaying these animalistic tendencies. It may be an inmate in a top security jail for extremely violent offenders who needs to be restrained by eight prison guards because even though he is not physically big he can generate massive force. Or it may be a madman in a lunatic asylum who goes into a rage and needs eight staff to restrain him.

They may be different people in different situations but they will both have the same physical manifestations, thrashing, clawing, shouting, wild eyed rage.

One can only assume that in ancient times in mainland china these phenomner were noticed and the Old Yang Style of Taiji is a system that was designed specifically to bring about this transformation. It also of course contains all the internal qi gong to improve our health so that even if we never need to use our training to defeat opponents we will have a great self healing benefit from our training.

We need the capacity to suddenly unleash our internal power because if we are in a relatively passive state of mind walking down the street and the opponent has been preparing himself, getting his adrenalin pumping and his mind focused on attacking us, we are at a big disadvantage. If he leaps out at us and we stay in our normal human frame of mind, how can we cope with his massively increased stature and force. Most normal people would be over whelmed and defeated but our taiji teaches us to go from normal to berserk rage in an instant.

We would be meeting them with a greater amount of force than they ever expected was possible in a person. This is because it is the animal within that does the fighting for us. The normal human mind does not have the will or the inclination for such barbarity and brutality but the animal within only knows that it needs to survive and will do whatever is necessary to achieve that.

Some people naturally have access to this extreme yang qi potential and the taiji training gives them a way to control and channel this power. Others are so distant from this side of themselves that it takes years of training for them to access this inner power. A person with an excessive nature will be regulated and restrained by the taiji training and a person with a lack of vitality and expression will be invigorated by it and be able to achieve great things they previously thought were beyond them.

We need to cover one final aspect of fighting and that is, the end of the fight. How will it end and what to do now, these things are very important and not often discussed. If you have not been able to avoid being attacked and have not been able to win and are left for dead then as soon as possible assess yourself and your situation. Is the danger over ? if not should you try to move or play dead ? if the attacker has gone and the immediate danger has passed then check your injuries if you can. Have you been stabbed, the majority of people do not realise at the time that they have been stabbed.

Check and see, stem the blood loss if you can, get help as soon as you can, there may be major internal bleeding that is not obvious at first. Try and remember as much as you can about the attacker so that you can give the information to the law enforcement officers.

Whilst we are discussing knife attacks it is worth mentioning that the overwhelming majority of people who survive an attack and are able to recount what happend say that they did not know the opponent had a knife. So we have to assume that the opponent has a knife and we have to therefore be prepared for a fight to the death encounter.

If the attacker is not armed and turns out to be inferior to us and we are able to defeat them with out hurting them then we can feel good within ourselves and we can know that we have not only won the fight but also won the moral high ground.

However if we are the recipient of an unprovoked attacked on the street by a crimminal who is intent on robbing us after he has stabbed us to death then we are in big trouble if our mind set was one that focused on bieng on the moral high ground. We would not be able to defend ourselves and our attempt to hold the moral high ground would result in us ending up in a coffin under the ground.

It makes more sense to assume the worst case senario and if we train to be able to cope with this, then if it is a lesser situation, we are going to be more than able to deal with it. We train Taiji as a fighting art because it is better to have it and not need it than not have it when you need it.

So if the fight is over and you have lost and have thoughts of revenge, then use the power of that as a force to mobilise you to fight your way to a full recovery. Then get back to training, learn from the experience so that if there is a next time you can be the winner.

If you are the winner of the fight and you have done whatever was necessary to survive on the street then you need to finish the fight. The opponent attacked you because he wanted to steal something from you, your possessions, your money your health, your life. You have every reason to show no mercy and have no regrets about your actions. If you are married and have children and the opponent had killed you then not only have you lost your life but the life of your partner and children has been destroyed as well. The crimminal madman who attacked you would have deprived a child of a parent and a husband or wife of a partner.

The attacker is doing more than attacking you, indirectly he is attacking your family. If you have trained your taiji enough then when the opponent attacked, you should have hit him many times and he should be unconscious before he hits the ground. If he is not then it is essential that you hit him whilst he is down, if you don't then they might get up again re attack and kill you.

How you hit them when they are down and where is the most important thing. It is essential to not kick them in the head for a number of reasons, firstly because the whole fight has probably been recorded on close circuit security cameras. If the case went to court even though you were the one who was originally attacked the video footage of you kicking a man in the head when he is on the ground could turn the verdict against you.

Secondly because his hands will naturally be near his head to protect it, if you go to kick him in the head he could grab your foot and drag you down to the ground. Thirdly we are hitting him whilst he is down to stop him getting up and re attacking. So the only sure way to do this is to stamp on his ankle.

He will be expecting you to kick his head not his ankle so he will not be prepared for it or ready to defend against it. After you have stamped or jumped on his ankle he will not be able to stand up, so if you run away he cannot chase after you.

This is very very important, the last thing you want is to have achieved the great success of surviving being attacked by a thug, to have knocked him down to the ground and then him getting up again chasing you down and beating you up or killing you.

So we train taiji all our lives as a martial art so that we have the ability to defend our family and friends and ourselves. It can give us the edge that we need if we are ever in a physical confrontation but hopefully we will never have to use it.

So instead we find that all the side effects of the training have enhanced our lives. Our mind and emotions are more steady and balanced, our bodies are healthier and stronger and we have more energy, more self confidence and a greater chance for a longer happier life.

Chapter 12
Dim Mak

The Tai Chi Classics say that Dim Mak should not be taught to criminals or people who are not loyal or who are not from a good background. Nor should it be taught to people with evil intentions or those who are carless and crude. It should not be explained to those who have no concideration for others or those who pretend to be polite but are realy not compassionate. Only if a person is reliable and has a good memory and emotional stability should they be considered as a possible student for dim mak.

Dim mak means hitting the acupuncture points, to cause disorientation, weakness and collapse, temporary or permanent paralysis, unconsciousness or death. Different results are possible depending on which point or combination of points are hit and how they are hit. One of the most commonly asked questions about this aspect of taji is because the points are so small how can you hit them in the turmoil of a fight ? To be able to hit an acupuncture point only seems like a hard thing to do if people have not trained in the Old Yang Style of Taiji.

Every thing that we do is designed to position us so that we can easily hit these points on the opponent. As soon they move towards us we move towards them and strike straight away. The Tai Chi Classics describe this as striking the incoming energy. And that to make it work we should be like a speeding horse destroying all in its path. If we hit the points as a pre emptive move the classics say that this is called striking the contained energy. The classics say that to make this work we need to have the ferocity of a tiger pouncing on sheep.

We have a moment where we connect with their arms it is here as a result of all our training that we know where, purely through touch, the various points we need to hit are. We just slide up along the arm and will inevitable find the head, neck and torso. We never have to look for the points, the taiji moves are all designed to cause us to land on a point however the encounter develops.

At a high level because we are so familiar with the location of the points and how to get to them subconsciously with out any effort or conscious thought we are able to just hit the points on the opponents torso head and neck even if we do not have a connection on their arms to guide us in first.

There are actually a few misunderstandings about dim mak that need to be clarified, there is a belief that dim mak is the delayed death touch. Yes there are some points that when hit cause the person to die days weeks or months or years later but these points are not the whole dim mak system, just a small part of it. When we are fighting for our lives we want to save our lives and if that means having to take their life straight away then we do it. There is no point in being killed and going to the grave knowing that you will soon be joined by your assailant. Much better is to send him on his way to the next world and stay in this one and enjoy a long happy life in good health.

The delayed aspect is often a medical phenomena, for example there is a point that we hit because under it is an important blood vessel that we are trying to crush. If we hit it correctly a small section of the interior wall of the artery will eventually detach itself and get carried to the brain (embolus) where it will cause a clot resulting in a stroke and death.

There is also another point that when hit fractures another blood vessel which bleeds directly into the brain (cerebral haemorrhage) , causing coma and death some time later. These delayed death strikes are a result of structural damage because of the anatomy of the human body according to western medicine.

This next explanation sounds very hard to believe to people who have been only educated to see the body the western way. There are also certain fa jin dim mak strikes which work because of the anatomy of the human body according to Chinese medicine. We strike with such devastating force that the shockwave of the fa jin qi penetrates deep into the body along the meridian system until it reaches the internal organ and creates major damage resulting in a blockage and stagnation of their energy that over time causes the functional power of their internal organs to get weaker and then fail. So weeks later they die, depending on what point you hit and how you hit it, they will have heart or lung or kidney failure etc.

Also there is another misunderstanding about dim mak, some people still think that we have to hit certain points at certain times of day. Yes there are points that work slightly better at a particular time of day but the vast majority of acupuncture points that we use for dim mak work all the time.

Many people also believe that one needs to know about the creative and destructive cycle of the five elements theory of Traditional Chinese Medicine to be able to use dim mak correctly.

Again this is not the case, all one needs to know is the location of the point and the direction of the strike (up, down, left or right) and whether to rotate the strike clockwise or anti clockwise to cause an energy drainage effect, also of course one needs to have fa jin. These things are learnt as a subconscious reflex by the body through training the Old Yang Style System.

Fa jin has many levels and so does dim mak, the higher the level of fa jin one is at, the higher level of dim mak one can apply. It is possible on many of the dim mak points to get them to work even without fa jin, just with a normal external strike, others need to be hit with the great penetrating power that can only come from the basic waist shaking left, right, left or right, left, right fa jin movement.

When we get to the higher levels of fa jin where we are releasing a sort of electrical shock charge into the opponent then we can use certain other points that only respond to this electrical charge or the same basic points but get a bigger result with less effort.

Some people are confused and believe that you can go straight to the advanced fa jin energy shock attack just with breathing training and some meditation or qi gong. This is not the case, one has to get into all the basic combat contact training stuff first, the large and small san sau, long har chuan and single and double push hands as well as the taiji fight sequence applications from the whole system.

A person has to be able to fight first and then after a few years of giving and receiving punches and kicks, bruises and blood then the high levels of fa jin and dim mak are attainable, there are no short cuts on this journey !!

It is important to remember that we are training a martial art, taiji is not a dance, it is a practical fighting system. There are some training methods that we have were we get hit. This is a good thing because it is important to desensitise the body to the physical and mental shock of being hit and also of hitting someone else. We are not hitting hard enough to cause any major damage but we are hitting hard enough to make the body think its for real.

And last of all one of the biggest confusions is about the so called death touch, yes it is possible but it is not a touch it is a fa jin strike delivered with great force. You cannot kill someone with a touch, the reason that this misunderstanding has grown is that to an onlooker the strike was so small and quick that it just looked like a touch.

At the high level of fa jin we can deliver the blow from touch contact with the opponent, we don't have to draw back our arm to hit them but because this is not understood, it is inevitable that the incorrect conclusion has been drawn and it is thought that there was just a touch not a strike. So dim mak should really be translated as death strikes or strikes to acupuncture points that can cause death not the death touch.

We can of course do many other things with our fa jin dim mak apart from kill the opponent, we can temporarily or permanently paralyse his limbs or we can knock him out or drain his energy so he collapses. It is the ability to knock people out that I think is the best aspect of fa jin dim mak to develop. This is because when we are attacked our main motivation is to stop the opponent from attacking us, the most sensible way to do this is with a knock out.

Some other martial arts hit the opponent continuously till the pain he is experiencing becomes unendurable and he stops attacking. This way of fighting takes some time so we don't use it, we need to be quick in case there is another opponent. Also some people can take a lot of pain and it does not stop them from attacking, in a fight people are so pumped up with yang energy that they often don't know that they have been hit or that they are in pain.

Another way to stop an attacker is to cause major trauma to his leg at the knee joint with a kick from the forty five degree angle, obviously if he can't stand up he can't fight. This is however you intentionally causing him a major physical crippling mutilation. When you can just knock him out, it seems unnecessary to break his body in to pieces.

So obviously you cannot always choose which points you are going to hit, so you just hit whatever points the opponent gives you access to. It is however legally and morally better to try and cause knock out rather than death. If you have the choice, choose not to damage the opponent more than is necessary to stop them fighting you. It may happen that a mad drugged up criminal decides to stab you to death and you only get one chance to counterattack and the only point you have access to is a death point. Well in a kill or be killed situation you do what is necessary to survive.

It is because of the knock out that another legend has crept into the taiji story, people say that they were knocked out and the taiji fighter never touched them. What really happened was the fa jin was to fast to see and with a knock out the person who has been hit, upon recovering consciousness has lost the memory of the second just before he went into knock out. So of course they did not see the strike land or recall the feeling of the blow so they inevitably jump to the conclusion that it never landed and then they say that they were knocked out without being touched and so another myth is created.

There are many acupuncture points that acupuncturists do not use because they are on vulnerable parts of the body, these are of course the points we use for dim mak. Some points can be used for both acupuncture and dim mak and some points are in reality never used for dim mak only acupuncture.
So points that are located over major blood vessels or points that are right on top of a major internal organ or points that are located on major nerves are all of course used as dim mak points. Also there are some points that are located on structural weak points in the body like the joints and the spine and certain areas of the skull, these are all targeted.

Of course points that are on or near the obvious commonly used target areas of all the martial arts are also attacked, neck, throat, eyes, groin and solar plexus. So it is clear that dim mak is based on a clear understanding of anatomy, there is no mystery.

Some people promote the idea that there is a mystery and try and incourage a wow! factor about dim mak, there is no mystery, it is just common sense to use all ones strength, the fa jin, against the opponents weakest areas, their dim mak points.

There are still some martial arts instructors who are not very well medically educated who actually show knock outs at demonstrations and the audience goes wow and are amazed and then the students are encouraged to practice knockouts on each other.

The first reason why I think this is strange is that, if for example an instructor said to a student, stand still with your legs open facing me. And then kicked them as hard as they could between the legs and as a result they fell to the ground and went unconscious or were so incapacitated that they could not get up again. Everyone would think that the instructor was acting irresponsibly and certainly no one would be impressed or amazed or go wow. They would just think get this poor student some medical help.

However if a martial arts instructor asks a student to stand in front of them and then hits them hard, not with fa jin, just a normal punch to the neck on a certain acupuncture point and as an inevitable result the poor student collapses unconscious to the floor and the instructor says 'that was the amazing dim mak point striking' then every one goes wow and thinks its all amazing. Even worse than this is that students are then incouraged to go of and hit each other, until everyone at the seminar has been knocked unconscious.

There are no teams of medical personnel standing by and no one knows why a knock out has occurred, if they did know what was the cause (nerve, heart and brain damage) they would never let it be done to them. There is short and long term damage from any type of knock out and it should only be used for defeating opponents not for demonstration.

To me there is no difference between a kick in the groin and a dim mak strike in the neck, they are both to weak points on the body and both cause serious and permanent damage. The point I am making is that we train martial arts for many reasons one of which is so that in a confrontation we do not get as seriously injured as we might have. So to unnecessarily invite the potentially fatal damage that can be done by a knock out to the neck is counter productive. If you are at a class, workshop or seminar and people are being knocked out don't let them do it to you. Not to the neck or any other points on the body.

The Old Yang Style System has been very cleverly designed so that it is possible to practice fa jin and dim mak in such a way that one can become effective in its use but not damaged in the training.

We train so that if we encounter the worst situation we have something to call upon. We hope for the best and prepare for the worst. A person who chooses to train the whole of the Old Yang Style Taiji System will eventually get to the very high levels which are more to do with energy rather than just physical force.

At the highest level we still hit the opponent but we are able to actually deliver into them a shockwave of adverse energy which we can guide with our intention along their acupuncture meridian channels deep into the most vulnerable parts of their body like their heart and brain causing instant death. This is extreme but better to have it and not need it, than not have it when you need it.

From a healing perspective the ability to put our energy into a specific part of another persons body is a great skill. We would of course use positive healing energy not adverse damaging energy. There are not two types of qi energy, good and bad. It is the same energy we just give it an adverse or healing intention depending on the circumstances. For healing we would be tapping into our spiritual nature not our animal nature.

The way to make our Taiji a system for tapping into the spiritual is to practice the long form very very slowly and include within it all the qi gong methods that are explained in the chapter on internal power.

Chapter 13
Fa jin

Fa jin is a whole body shaking explosion of qi, all the things that I describe in this book are part of fa jin but are not it in its entirety because Fa jin is greater than the sum of its parts. By doing all the things I explain you will be creating the right environment for fa jin to happen. And when it does happen all the different components that I describe will be happening within it.

If a person trains regularly then a sort of critical mass is reached and fa jin begins to happen by itself. How long it will take to reach this stage varies from person to person but once true fa jin has been activated then the purpose and use of taiji becomes clear. The use of taiji for defeating opponents and for improving ones health is a result of the fa jin energy, just slow flowing movements are not enough. If people only practice soft, slow taiji without any fa jin they may in fact become to soft and slow and weaken their mind and body.

Whether one is training in the old yang style of taiji for health or as a martial art, fa jin is the heart of the system. We have certain clearly defined physical things we have to do when we fa jin but at the higher levels fa jin is a result of the build up of internal energy demanding to be released through the martial applications.

When beginners try to hit some one without fa jin it is just with the fist or foot and they tend to make a big effort without getting much effect. With fa jin it is a whole body movement and there is a big result with little effort.

Yang Lu Chans Old Yang Style Taiji Long Form is the best place to develop fa jin. To begin with we do the whole form slowly then we make certain moves big fa jin with slap steps. At the most advanced level all the other moves are small shaking fa jins with shuffle steps and vibrating palms. We develop fa jin in this form then use it in every other aspect of the whole system.

Every taiji movement should be fa jin (explosive), even the slow taiji movements are just what fa jin would look like if it was slowed down. So really the performance of taiji slowly is just to get everything correctly positioned so that it is going to work smoothly when taken up to fa jin pace.

It is through practising the form slowly that beginners build up the qi till they have enough to fa jin. If one spends longer accumulating energy then it will be possible to fa jin sooner, if one rushes to try and do fa jin it will take longer to get it.

We also have to start with big movements and then go smaller with our movements because we can only increase power slowly over decades, it cannot be rushed. A good visual metaphor is if we first make a big box and fill it with a big spring then we have all the pieces in place. Next if we gradually shrink just the box and also strengthen it as we shrink it, then we have eventually got a situation where we have a big spring in a small box, which is strong enough to contain that potential energy and explosive power. To fa jin we open the box and release some of the accumulated qi.

So we first practice all our taiji moves as big open circles and then we slowly make the circles smaller and smaller over the following twenty years. If a person was thinking of a short cut and wanted to begin with small circles, this would be like just having a small spring in a small box, no potential power is present. No true internal fa jin can be developed and you have something which looks like advanced taiji but has no substance. To rush it and make the moves into small circles in just a year or two would mean that we have not built up a very powerful big spring and we have not given the box, our body, long enough to increase its strength to cope with containing increased internal power.

The development of true taiji internal power is a long and subtle processes, to rush forwards will set you back. To build up fa jin through cultivating the taiji principles and internal qi gong, to develop true internal power, is like growing an oak tree, it takes decades and is a slow organic process.

It is my personal belief that if a person practised taiji but never developed fa jin it would be like an archer only ever drawing his bow but never firing an arrow. Continuous slow movement is not enough to really invigorate the energy and blood circulation to maintain health. Only fa jin can really rush the blood and qi around the body at a vigorous enough pace to clear away stagnation and invigorate the functional power of all the internal organs.

The development of all of taiji's internal qi gong and principles of structure and movement are there to eventually get us to the highest level of fa jin. If a person does not pursue this goal and never gets to the high level of fa jin but has mastered some of the internal principles, then they will still have some small benefits for their health, but will never understand the true use of taiji as a martial art. And the possible great health benefits are unlikely to ever be fully gained.

So the Old Yang Style Long Form is the best place to learn how to fa jin, first we learn the movements then we put into them various internal principles to incourage the development of fa jin. The first set of internal principles to be put into the form to create the right environment for fa jin could be called Internal Principles of Posture.

Internal Principles of Posture

We have the feet clawing the ground whenever they touch it and we have the knees slightly bent to lower the centre of gravity. This feels like as if you were sitting on a horse. We have the spine straight and vertical like the sky reaching trunk of a pine tree. At a more advanced level we have a 'C' shaped back and at the highest level we have a straight back with just the feeling of a 'C' shaped back. The feeling is like as if you were carrying a turtle shell on your back.

The tongue is on the roof of the mouth, the shoulders are relaxed and down, the armpits have a space under them and the arms are in a just unlocked shape as if hugging a large tree trunk. The arms feel like they are hanging from the spine in the same way that a branch hangs from a tree trunk. The hands are very slightly stretched and concave and feel like claws.

We have a few alignments in our posture to help the body work as a single integrated unit, the nose is over the navel and the shoulders connect with the hips. We have the elbows connect with the knees and the hands and feet move together. We have the Hip Power go directly to the elbows as if they were physically connected together, so if the hip goes forward or back so does the same side elbow. We also always have one hand on the centre line and the other aligned with the elbow over the knee.

Once a person has got these basic alignments correct then they can practice the basic way of fa jin. We shake the hips left, right, left or right, left, right and this movement generates first a centrifugal momentum which throws the hands out and then a centre pedal motion which brings them back in. This is the basic way of fa jin striking, we use the rotational force of the hips to move the hands for us rather than moving them with the muscles of the upper body. The second set of internal principles to be added on top of this could be called Internal Principles of Movement, which are all explained in the next chapter on Internal Power.

Internal Principles of Movement

Yin - Yang and Qi
Earth Qi and Leg Power
Hip and Ribcage Rotation and Torque Force
Scapular Spring Torque Force
Abdominal Breathing
Opening and Closing the Kwa
Tendon Jin Elastic Force
Joint Sinew Jin Force
Bone Breathing
Spine Jin Power
Intention Force
Yin Yang Palm Power
Smooth Circular Spiralling Power
Loose Heavy Power
Rooting
Centrifugal and Centrepetel Power Waist Rotation
Lower and Upper Body Integrated Movement
Whole Body Power
Counter Torque Power
Connection Flowing Power
'C' Back Power
Squeezing Chi Power
The Qi Wave
Martial Mind Power

We also need to understand how to manage the movement of the mind and emotions. If the attack causes fear, anxiety and anger then this emotional energy needs to be released into the fa jin to add to its power. We need to know how to make use of the breathing, normal upper abdominal breathing, reverse lower abdominal breathing and both together. As well as whole body bone breathing and particularly spine breathing and palm breathing.

When the breathing has reached a high level one feels that on the inhalation the following acupuncture points move closer to the lower dan dien in the centre of the belly. Governing meridian point 20 and Conception meridian point 1, Governing meridian point 4 and Conception meridian point 4, Kidney meridian point1 and pericardium meridian point 8. And as you exhale these points all move away from the centre.

The eyes must be used correctly to create a sensation of pressure in the back of the head, which is the activation of the brain stem for reflex fighting. The eye movement, gaze left and look right, gaze right and look left is combined with a Yang intention in the eyes, all these need to be coordinated with the Opening and Closing movements of all the Kwa. Working in a perfectly synchronised way with the hand circles manifest from the hip rotation and the wrist qi flow reflecting the dan dien qi flow.

So if we have all the Internal Principles of Posture working and all the Internal Principles of Movement operating smoothly then we can develop all three levels of fa jin striking. The first level of fa jin is the basic shift the weight and shake the waist, left right left or right left right type of big fa jin. We imagine the body (spine) is like a tree trunk and the arms and legs are like branches that come from it, so we shake the trunk and the branches are moved. This type of big fa-jing is like a tiger impacting with its prey, we use it with a slap step to cover the distance to the opponent.

The second more advanced and more internal type is the small double shaking fa jin which is like a snake striking. We use this with a shuffle step when we have closed the gap and need to adjust ourselves to the opponents slightest movement when we are standing next to them.

For the small double shaking fa jin there is more shaking of the waist and hips so we have the ability to hit the same dim mak acupuncture points twice with each strike. The movement is so sudden that an observer who did not know what they were supposed to be looking for would only see one strike and not the second strike to the same point straight after.

When a guitar string is plucked once it not only goes up and down once but has a second and even a third up and down movement as the energy of the string slowly releases itself. There is one big vibration and then smaller and smaller ones as the energy expends itself. It is the same with fa jin there is a type of residual waist shake after the main one and an even smaller one after that. The wrists, hands and fingers are all connected to the dan dien in the belly and so they reflect the bodies shaking movement and strike repeatedly to the same point.

The third set of internal principles to be put into the form to create the right environment for things like the advanced vibrating palm touch contact fa jin could be called Internal Principles of Intention.

Internal Principles of Intention

If we imagine that the body is a weapon like the archers bow, then the bow is the body, the elasticity of the bow string with the power it supplies to the arrow is the qi and the sharpness of the arrow is the intention. We began with principles to align the body and then with qi gong to develop the internal power and last of all we work with Intention.

At this advanced level intention leads the qi which will lead the body. So to hit the opponent we are no longer thinking anything about what to do with the body, how to move it or where to move it to, we just have an intention and everything else does itself.

Our advanced fa jin is like a sudden bolt of lightning or an electrical discharge. Some people find it hard to imagine that we can carry with us an electrical charge. We all can give someone a static electric shock as we touch them and in taiji we use a flowing natural way of moving to build up our charge so we can have a bigger effect than just a little shock.

An electric eel can knock a man unconscious with its electrical discharge, we are not biologically the same as an eel but after many years of training when we hit someone at the high level on a dim mak point with fa jin we are doing more than just physically smashing a nerve centre.

We are releasing a shockwave of electromagnetic force into their energy channels and getting it to disrupt the smooth function of their internal electrical systems, like the brain and heart. We can cause knock out and death through guiding the electrical bomb of fa jin deep into their bodies and getting it to detonate inside their internal organs.

This and other advanced fa jin abilities do not result from the practice of an additional training method, rather it is a result of years of just training the whole system correctly. We get to the advanced touch contact fa fin level by having the intention of doing the small double shaking fa jin but not actually physically doing them. So the same shockwave of qi is released inside us and travels along the same pathways within the body to be released in our strike not because we actually physically do the double hip shake but as a result of us just having the intention of doing it.

The best way to explain it would be to say that the train charging through the tunnel is the fa jin and the tunnel itself is the body, you cannot see the train in the tunnel but the tunnel shakes a bit as the train powers through. So you feel a massive force blasting through you but you are not really moving, as the fa jin shudders through you the arm and hand vibrate slightly, but the force is on the inside internally vibrating, so this type of touch contact fa jin is very powerful but cannot be seen.

The application of these touch contact fa jin is different to the other types. With big fa jin you can see the movement of the body and the hand travels a distance as you leap at the target. With the small double shaking fa jin the blow can be delivered over as short a distance as one inch when you are right next to the person and the same point is hit twice at the same time.

With the touch contact fa jin no distance is travelled, you only have to be able to touch the target point and you can hit it. We use this for the delivery of the most devastating dim mak strikes against grapplers from no distance. Grapplers close the distance very quickly and hug you closely because they think you will not have room to hit them from such a close range. They then take you to the ground where they can make the best use of their art.

However taiji is designed to defeat grapplers, first we hit them before the fight begins or if it has begun then as they close the distance we hit them. We are able to do this because we do not have to draw back our fist or foot prior to striking, if we did we would have wasted our opportunity and they will be on us. As they move we move and strike with fa jin to dim mak points and then we move and strike with fa jin to dim mak points again and again.

If we have missed all these opportunities and they have covered the distance and are beginning their hug and are just about to sweep or throw us to the ground, we hit them. We are able to hit them because we can touch them and that is all we need with our advanced fa jin.

An aspect of this touch contact fa jin which manifests at a high level is a slight visible shaking of the hand but you are not shaking the hand, it feels like all the bones in the hand are vibrating. When you have finished the form and the vibrating palm is no longer visible on the outside you can still feel it for a while on the inside. This vibrating palm fa jin is what we use on touch contact electrical dim mak strikes.

Touch contact fa jin means as you touch the opponent you release the internal vibrating fa jin into them, you do not need to cover any distance to build up speed or momentum. Touch contact fa jin is a devastatingly powerful way of delivering the dim mak strike and also what we need to have to use taiji the way it was designed to be used for defeating opponents from very close range with no preliminary movement. We don't have to pull the hip or the hand back, we don't have to get ready to do it. The potential energy is always there, we just have the intention and its done.

At an advanced level all the applications are from no distance because he is rushing towards you to hit you and you rush towards him to close the distance even more and then you are there right next to him. They cannot kick you because you are to close and they cannot punch you because you are within there arms length. Here we use knees, shoulders, elbows, forearms and head butts with crushing effectiveness.

If the taiji fighting tactics have been correctly applied then you should be standing just behind their shoulder. It is from here that, from no distance you use touch contact fa jin, to deliver the deadly dim mak attacks. Last of all one of the fatal finishing moves are applied. These have the finality of a guillotine coming down on an unprotected neck.

The Old Yang Style Way of Fighting may seem gruesome in the extreme but if you have tried to avoid a fight and have been chased into a dead end ally and are trapped with no hope of escape or rescue. Then when facing a gang of hardened criminals armed with knives and iron bars what are you going to do ?

Long range kicking techniques are not going to help when there is no long range left, they are rushing in. Grappling techniques are of no help because as soon as you go to the ground with one of them the rest who are standing up will kick you and stab you. Facing them and exchanging blows at arms length would be a big mistake if their blows were more numerous and powerful. So what we need to do is have a way of moving so we are not where they are attacking, so we can use our power not in blocking there attacks but in attacking them.

We are ruthless with the first opponent because we need to make sure that once defeated they will not rise up to reattack whilst we are fighting the second opponent, this is why we have finishing moves. It is hard to defeat one opponent, to beat two or three would be remarkable. So to stack the odds in our favour we make sure that we never have to fight the same person twice.

The above example is a very extreme case that is unlikely to ever happen and for the vast majority of people any form of physical confrontation is usually a very rare event. I wish that all readers of this book have long happy lives and never encounter any unnecessary violence at all. In this case all the training is never used and it just ends up being interesting for our minds and beneficial for our health.

Only if it is trained as a martial art will it help us change and grow into more sturdy and balanced individuals. When you no longer have anything to prove to yourself or others then you can help other people more effectively. When you have cultivated your own energy then you can give the excess away. This is a deeper reason for developing internal power through our martial arts training.

If we train taiji as a martial art it will make our bodies and minds stronger and we will have the confidence and ability to defeat others but we should in the long term be more concerned with healing others not fighting them. Our study of taiji should lead into the study of Acupuncture and Chinese Herbal Medicine.

Chapter 14
Internal Power

This chapter will explain how by working with the body and the qi together we can develop our internal power. There are various internal qi gongs that we do on each taiji movement when we are practising our forms to gain the internal power however when we are using our taiji for defeating opponents we just concentrate on hitting them. All the internal qi gongs are going to be happening anyway because we have made them subconscious.

There are many different internal qi gongs, although each one develops a different thing, they all have one thing in common and that is, they all generate and circulate qi. To begin with the qi gongs are quite rough then after many years of practice they sink in to the body and subconscious mind and are no longer visible, they are smooth and truly internal.

Sometimes in training we consciously emphasise one particular internal qi gong above the rest to become more familiar with it. At other times we just let the taiji do itself and it will re balance us in the way we need most at that time.

All the qi gongs overlap with each other in a variety of different ways. It is easier if they are learnt separately but eventually they all intertwine and happen together.

Qi means energy and gong means work so qi gong means working with energy. In it its finest frequency qi is a spiritual force that can change the world, it can also be looked at in a more straight forward way as being just like an electrical current, a magnetic field or a heat wave.

Interacting opposites are what is needed to generate energy, with electricity there is a positive and negative current, a magnet has a positive and negative side and heat is generated by the friction of two surfaces rubbing against each other in opposite directions.

So opposing and interacting opposites are the key elements for creating these forces and with qi it is the same except the two interacting opposites are called Yin and Yang. In taiji at an advanced level Yin and Yang are subtle abstract mental and spiritual forces that can be experienced but are very hard to convey to others, at a basic level they relate to simple tangible physical principles which can be explained in a reasonably straight forwards way.

Whether a person is training taiji to defeat opponents or for self development, self healing or healing others or to develop their spirituality and spiritual body, their ability to progress is dependent on their qi. The internal principles and qi gong that one learns as a beginner are mainly to do with physical things to create a Yin Yang dynamic to generate qi. I will categorise them into Yin and Yang but of course nothing is just Yin or Yang because they are always transforming into each other so they always contain a bit of one another.

Earth Qi and Leg Power

The first qi gong is to push against the ground with the foot in a circular way, the body here is Yang and the Earth Yin. The second way is to have one leg push against the other, the pushing leg is Yang and the receiving leg is Yin and then they reverse. This compression and release is another Yin Yang way of generating qi. It is just like when a spring is compressed it is given potential energy that it then releases which compresses the other leg and so on. So qi is constantly being stored and released by the legs.

We have the body internally connected by the internal structure that we cultivate in our taiji training and it is through this 'Way of Being Internally Connected' that the qi from the legs which begins from the ground force can be carried up through the body and be released through the palms of the hands. If we release the qi in our fa jin with the intention of a hawk impacting with its prey then our dim mak attacks will be effective. If we release the qi through ourselves into a patient whilst having our intention at one with nature and an open and compassionate heart then a great healing is possible.

Kidney meridian point 1 on the sole of the foot is associated with Water and Pericardium point 8 in the palm of the hand is associated with Fire so if we train barefoot on the grass and breath in and out through and K-1 and P-8 we can keep the qi balanced. Any excesses heat which is generated by our Qi gong is absorbed by the ground and the cool Yin energy of the earth helps to keep us mentally and emotionally calm.

Traditionally it is said that the fa jin qi is emitted from the hands out of P-8 and with fa jin kicks the qi is emitted out of K-1. It is also written in the classics that earth qi is absorbed up into the body through K-1 as long as it does not touch the ground when our feet are on the ground. This is achieved by having the feet claw the ground whenever they touch it.

Hip and Ribcage Rotation for Torque Force

Moving up the body the next internal principle is the Yin Yang change of the waist (by this I mean the pelvis, sacram and hip bones and lower abdomen as one single unit) turning one way then the other. This waist shake is one of the main sources for fa jin, to begin with waist shaking fa jin is big however at the advanced level it is very small and becomes a very concentrated 'Small Internal Fa Jin'. The continuous waist turning twist generates qi and activates the Lower Dan Dien energy centre just below and behind the navel in the centre of the belly.

The Lower Dan Dien is both an electrical generator of qi and a rechargeable battery. Also the centrifugal Yang and centre pedal Yin forces generated by the waist rotation cause the qi to be flowed from the belly to the extremities and back again.

The torque of the hips in opposition to the rib cage is a Yin upper body, Yang lower body compression release that generates qi through its twisting contrary movement. This is an internal principle that should not be exaggerated to much otherwise it causes a break between the upper and lower body. It is important to remember to keep the lower body sturdy and substantial- a Yang state and the upper body loose and elastic- a yin state. This interaction of opposites regulates and balances the qi and adds to our power.

Squeezing Qi Power

Another upper body - lower body Yin Yang qi generating technique is the bringing together and the moving apart the hip bone and lateral side of the floating rib. This Yin Yang compression release is called 'Squeezing Qi' because the qi that is generated causes the striking hand to be squeezed full of the qi that has been created by the movement, it also causes the arm that is striking to extend the necessary extra distance.

Scapular Spring Torque Force

There are three main torque force components, the waist (hips-dan dien), the ribcage and the scapular. We first turn the waist, a moment later this turns the ribcage and last of all the scapular are moved. The waist then turns back followed by the ribcage and then the scapular. Most people have their scapular almost stuck onto their backs and have very little movement with them. Once they are activated and loosened up they become more movable and can be made to stick out and look like wings.

The arms connect directly to the scapular, one is Yang and the other is Yin. So when one scapular is forwards its arm will also be forwards and the other scapular will be back and out and its arm will be in. This in out movement of the arms from the scapular is like loading and releasing a spring mechanism of great power.

The arms are being held by the scapular so we are able to relax the shoulders even more so that there is less tension and more qi can flow. When this movement is working smoothly the arms shoot out one then the other and there is a corresponding rising and falling of the scapular in and out on the back, their rolling movement massages acupuncture points which are used to heal the heart and lungs.

When these three torque components are all activated and working smoothly then the feeling is as if the scapular where rolling around on the ribcage which itself is rolling over a big ball of qi (the lower dan dien) which sits in the pelvis.

Abdominal Breathing

The Yin-Yang, in-out, compression-release of the abdominal breathing techniques that we use in our taiji also generate qi and pumps it from the lower dan dien to the extremities. Beginners use Upper Abdominal Breathing, this strengthens one,s Acquired Qi (the energy we get from food and air). The chest does not rise up, it stays relaxed and down. When we inhale while moving the hands down or towards our bodies, we allow the area between the solar plexus and the navel to expand.

When we exhale while moving the hands up or away from the body, we allow this area to contract. This breathing does not involve any muscle tension. It is all accomplished by mental intention. Do not force anything, just keep the mouth closed and breath through the nose slowly and calmly.

Advanced level practitioners are using Reverse Lower Abdominal Breathing. This strengthens one's Inherited Qi (the energy you are born with). When we inhale while moving the hands down or towards our bodies, we allow the area between the navel and the pubic bone to contract. When we exhale while moving the hands up or away from the body, we allow this area to expand. We keep the mouth closed and breath through the nose. Each breath should be calm, deep and slow. This breathing should not be forced but allowed to happen of itself.

There is no muscle tension involved, everything is accomplished by mental intention. The movements of the body are totally integrated with the breathing, which should be as long, slow and smooth as possible. Our breathing should be so quiet that even we cannot hear it. With Reverse Lower Abdominal Breathing, the kicks are done on the inbreath.

The most advanced technique is on each breath to do Upper Abdominal Breathing and at the same time to also do Reverse Lower Abdominal Breathing. So when we inhale and the hands come down or towards our bodies, the lower abdomen comes in and the upper abdomen out. When we exhale and the hands go up or away from our bodies the lower abdomen goes out and the upper abdomen in. An additional advanced technique when doing this type of breathing is to inhale and hold the breath for a second before exhaling.

Opening and Closing the Kwa

There is another type of breathing using the Kwa, it is not the expansion and contraction of the lungs but the expansion and contraction of the body. With the Kwa we have Yin compression and Yang release, the 'Opening (Yang) and Closing (Yin)' of all the 'Kwa' is also a major generator of qi. This movement feels like the whole body is breathing.

There is the Hand Kwa, Arm Kwa, Leg Kwa, Foot Kwa, Back Kwa and Pelvic Kwa. They can become such a powerful qi pumping process that ones qi expands and fills the body out like a balloon being inflated and even more than this our defensive qi on the surface is expanded significantly as well reinforcing our resistance to disease. Having strong defensive qi helps us in combat against opponents and also helps our immune system fight off illness.

We use the Kwa (semi circular shapes like a bridge or an archers bow) to form the correct posture so that in our Taiji the body will be open to a great qi flow and have structural integrity. And we Open Yang and Close Yin, bend and straighten them to generate more qi and increase our internal power.

The hand Kwa is formed by having the hand concave and stretched long and wide and also by having the Dragons mouth open, this is the semi circle created between the thumb and index finger. We keep a space under the armpits and have our arms out in front of the body so that together they create a semi circle shape (like a horse shoe shape), this is the Arm Kwa, also known as the band of power.

The knees are bent with a feeling of a spring pushing outwards between the knees and the feet claw the ground so that the outside edges of the feet contact the ground and not the instep. Doing this creates the feeling of being bow legged, these things all combine to form the Leg Kwa. The feet claw the ground whenever they make contact with it and this curved shape of the foot is the Foot Kwa. The head is pulled up and the coccyx pulled under, this causes the spine to be slightly curved like a crescent moon, this is the Back Kwa.

The internal movement of Opening and Closing the Pelvic Kwa is like a butterfly, the pelvis is the butterflies wings and the sacrum is its body. Once the Opening and Closing of the Pelvic Kwa has been mastered then all of the other Kwa Open and Close naturally as a result of this. The eyes also 'Open' this means that they glare like a madmans eyes and 'Close' this means that they go thin like the venomous eyes of a snake.

When we inhale we are Opening and when we exhale we are Closing the Kwa. Also as you are opening you begin to close and visa versa plus at a higher level as the right side of the body is opening the left side is closing and visa versa.

The animal that most clearly shows this use of the internal survival power of the Opening and Closing of the Kwa is the Tiger. This great creature walks the taiji walk when it stalks its prey. It crouches 'Closes' and then leaps and 'Opens' all its Kwa, its Pelvic Kwa Opens, its Spine Kwa Opens, its Arm Kwa Opens (its front legs), its Leg Kwa Opens (its back legs), all four of its paws Open to release its claws (the Hand and Foot Kwa). It also Opens its eyes and jaws and roars.

On impact with its prey all the Kwa 'Close' at the same time, there is incredible local damage from its fangs and claws but more than this, the Closing movement of every part of the tigers body as it impacts with its prey causes a devastating traumatic shock. This is what happens to the opponent when we hit him. When one practices ones taiji at this level the whole body feels like a pair of giant jaws Opening and Closing. The feeling is like the whole body is breathing, like the whole body is One Kwa, Opening and Closing.

Another aspect of breathing with the Kwa is that the qi flow is very strong to every part of the body. As the qi expands it feels like one is expanding beyond oneself, beyond the confines of the physical body. The expansion of the Kwa causes one to expand out of oneself, looking down you can see the physical body doing the Taiji by itself, you are aware of it but viewing the world from a higher perspective.

If we are practising our fa jin correctly then because we have at least one residual waist shake after the main one there will also be at least one small opening and closing of the kwa after the main opening and closing movement. Also if the closing part of the fa jin movement has been applied with the correct amount of force then it will cause the feet to both be lifted of the ground.

In the Old Yang Style Long Form as well as each movement Opening and Closing the whole form also Opens and Closes. It begins Open, up to movement number 101 Leaping Double Front Kick where it Closes. Then it Opens again at movement number 160 Right Foot Slap Step Forwards and Squeeze Low - FAJING.

Tendon Jin Elastic Force

If we slightly flex the tendons (the bits that connect the muscles to the bones) this will attracted the qi to them so that they can grow and develop and contribute to our elastic Jin force that we use in our Fa Jin explosive movements. We still keep the muscles relaxed as much as is possible. By letting go of any unnecessary tension in the muscles it will allow a greater amount of qi to flow unrestricted through the body and help in the development of our Loose Heavy Power.

The elastic power of the tendons is like the force of a bow string, the fingertips are the arrow head but the penetrating power is supplied by the bow string, the tendons. They are continually stretched and released and over a few years we can actually see that the tendons have grown longer and stronger.

Joint Sinew Jin Force

We also work with an even more advanced internal aspect of qi generation called Joint Jin. It is the use of the expansion and contraction of the ligaments inside the joints between the bones, in the hips, knees, elbows, ankles, wrists, fingers, toes and in particular in the shoulders.

It is in the shoulders that we can most see the Joint Jin expanding and contracting aspect of fa jin, it gives one at least an extra five inches reach and the elastic resiliant Jin power of the ligaments on top of the elastic power of the tendons makes our explosive Fa Jin strikes devastating.

A person when shot by an arrow suffers an injury caused not by the arrow but by the power supplied to it by the bow string, it is the same with the body, it is not the fist that causes injury to the opponent but the power supplied to it by the elastic resilient expanding and contracting qualities of the tendons and ligaments.

Bone Breathing

In the taiji when we inhale we expand the meridian qi out to support the defensive energy and when we exhale we contract the qi in to the bones, this is called 'Bone Breathing'. This expansion and contraction of the main meridian qi out to the defensive qi and in to the centre of the bones has three great benefits, firstly all the minute extra meridians have qi rushed through them so every part of the whole of the body is energised.

Secondly the compression of the qi into the bones makes them denser and regenerates the marrow which is a major part of the bodies blood production system, so this is good for general health and essential for longevity.

The third benefit is that when we exhale on contact with the opponent and sink our qi into the ground and in to our bones the impact generated is enough to cause the opponents system to go into shock and shut down, this is because contact impact power is related to momentum, which is speed plus weight.

The sinking of the body internally as we sink the qi into the bones at the same time causes a temporary weight increase on the point of contact. The body weight does not increase but the existing weight is concentrated more on the point of contact with the opponent.

The elastic release of the tendons and ligaments is the speed and the density of the bones is the weight, the two together make fa jin devastating. When 'Bone Breathing' is working the whole skeletal structure starts to vibrate, every bone in ones body is buzzing.

Spine Jin Power

We can combine Joint Sinew Jin Force and Bone Breathing in the spine to create Spine Jin Power. When we inhale the spaces between the vertebrae are expanded and when we exhale they are compressed. If done correctly this Yin - expansion and Yang - contraction of the spaces between the vertebrae of the spine causes the generation of a very powerful qi which then gathers at the middle of the spine and flows down the arms like a pulse on each movement into the palms of the hands.

It is healing for the spine and whole body because every nerve in the body begins in the spine and the wave of qi which flows outwards from the spine heals all the nerves. Also this spine breathing gives our fa jin qi release strikes more power. To fa jin from the spine correctly it must be straight and vertical like the trunk of a pine tree, when we shake the spine it causes the branches and leaves (arms and hands) to be moved.

Yin Yang Palm Power

The hands change from yin to yang, this means that the hand that was Yang would have the yin meridians on the palm stretched and the yang meridians on the back of the hand compressed. The other hand at this time would be the opposite, Yin, it would have the yin meridians on the palm compressed and the yang meridians on the back of the hand are stretched.

As one hand comes out of its Yang state and goes into its Yin state the other hand is coming out of its Yin state and going into its Yang state. The hands are continuously storing and releasing there yin and yang qi as we flow through the taiji movements whether it is for fighting or for healing.

When we are attacking an opponent with a palm strike the hand changes from yin to yang on contact and releases a penetrating shockwave of adverse yang qi into the acupuncture dim mak point. This yang qi is released from the yin part of the palm which goes slightly yang on contact. If one is practising fa jin correctly then each of the hands change from yin to yang and back again at least twice on each fa jin because we are shaking the hips/spine out and back and then the residual rebound energy causes it to shake at least one more time.

The healing benefit of having the Yin Yang palm power flowing is that it is actually the end of the wave of qi that has its origin in the Lower Dan Dien. So the whole body is having its yin and yang meridians balanced with each other in their correct pairs.

The correct practice of the Yin Yang Palm Power builds up the electromagnetic qi force around the hands to such a great level that the hands cannot touch one another, nor can the fingers of the same hand touch each other. The whole body feels like a giant charged magnet and the arms cannot touch the body and the legs cannot touch each other, no part of the body can touch another because the magnetic charge is just to great. It feels like being surrounded by a massive electrical field as if one were in a cocoon. This sensation of a force field emanating from the Lower Dan Dien out to the skin surface and beyond is very pleasant and increases the ability of the defensive qi to resist disease.

The Qi Wave

There are several waves of qi all flowing through the body at the same time. The first one is from the dan dien outwards to the hands feet and head, the second is from the earth up through the body and the third is from the coccyx up the spine to the head and down the arms.

The wave is an internal energy flow through the body, it can be exaggerated so that it becomes externalised and you can see a pulsation of movement going through the whole body and rolling all the way out to the finger tips. However like all of taiji's principles it needs to be internalised until only you can feel it and it is not externally obvious.

The qi wave flows through the Lower Dan Dien and causes the Yin Yang Hand to happen. The qi wave is partly from inside of the body and is also an external force that flows through us and mobilises the movement, it feels like being carried along by a wave in the ocean but you are also the wave.

This qi in the air is always there even though we are not usually aware of it. It is just like radio waves are all around us but we are not aware of them , then when we turn on the radio we can tune in and hear them. It is the same with the qi wave through the practice of taiji we can tune in and ride the wave.

The qi wave of the hips and dan dien causes a wave in the hands, on certain movements there is an almost physical ripple of qi along the top of the forearm as it flows down to the hand and out the fingers.

If we put the yin yang diagram on its side we see that the dividing line between yin and yang is a wave. So a combination of all the yin yang interactions mentioned so far results in the feeling of a ball of qi shaped like the Yin Yang diagram rotating in the belly.

This is the end result of years of dedicated training, one first learns were to put the hands and feet, then about turning the waist and then about the breathing and squeezing and opening and closing and all the other internal principles, so we are starting from the extremities and slowly getting closer to the centre.

One finds that once this high level has been reached of the yin yang qi ball rotating in the belly that all our movement is in fact a result of this. So we begin with the external movements to eventually mobilise the true internal power which we then find is what is really creating the external movement. So it is as with everything else a circle but when we return to where we began everything has changed and we are no longer the same person.

Intention Force

In our advanced training of the Old Yang Style Long Form the intention does the move and the hands are following but of course the intention has already finished the movement before the hands are even half way through it. So we don't then finish the move with our hands because we have already finished it with our qi which was following the intention. To actually complete the move with the hands would be to unnecessary waste qi which is counterproductive to the whole purpose of taiji.

So because of this process our form now looks different from a beginners version of the form, an observer would be able to see all of the movements that a begginer does. However our advanced form to an observer looks like we are not doing many of the movements and not completing the ones that we are doing. We are doing them all in full but we are doing them with our intention which others cannot see.

Chapter 15
Questions and Answers

There are certain taiji questions that I am often asked and I thought I would include them and my answers here.

Question.
Which is the best martial art ?

Answer.
It depends what aspects of yourself you want to develop, physical fitness, health, external power, internal power, striking, punching, kicking, throwing, locking, breaking, grappling/wrestling etc. Different styles emphasise different things. So no style is the best, it is just personal preference.

Question.
But which style will make me the best fighter ?

Answer.
Fighting and martial arts training are similar but different. To be a good martial artist you have to spend a lot of time training in the martial arts. To be a good fighter you have to go on to the street and fight. The difference is that a good fighter is a good fighter because of his state of being not because of how many martial arts techniques he knows.

For example if I was in a fight and I had a certain intention, if I decided I was going to kill the opponent, without any concern about the consequences of my actions, whether I go to jail for murder or whether I die in the fight. If I decided to use all the rest of my lifes available energy in this one confrontation, to have no rules, no fair fight, just to beat the opponent to death with my fists and feet or any weapon nearby, a bottle, a glass, a knife or an iron bar. If this was my state of being I would win every fight whether I knew martial arts or not.

And if the opponent did or did not know martial arts is also not as relevant as his state of being. If he was looking for a fair fight and had some self imposed limitations about what he was and was not prepared to do because of his concern about the consequences of his actions or because of a certain code of honour then he would loose.

Question.

Who would win if a practitioner of (name of one martial art) fought a practitioner of (name of another martial art) ?

Answer.

Its not the style which wins, its the man, in that moment, depending on his state of being. A good fighter can make their martial art work amazingly well even if they are only a beginner in that style.

A person who is not in the right state of bieng even if they have trained to the highest level of their martial art will still loose. Its the person who in that moment has the victory or the defeat not the style.

Question.

Is The Old Yang Style of Taiji good for self defence ? or for security staff ? or for police forces or for the army ?

Answer.

The Old Yang Style of Taiji was developed to kill the opponent so it would be good for the army but not appropriate for security staff or for the police force. If your life was in danger it could be used for self defence.

The reality of self defence is that we do not actually try and defend ourselves, if this is what we did then the attacker would continue to be the attacker and we would continue to be the victim, both physically and mentaly. The inevitable out come of this is that eventually one of his attacks gets through we are weakened, he exploits this weakness and grinds us into the ground, where we are then kicked to death.

So the only way to stop this is to turn the tables, we must become the attacker, as soon as we are attacked or even as soon as we are threatened with attack we should not hesitate but go on the offensive, the only way to win is to reverse the rolls.

They attack you and you don't defend yourself, you get out of the way of their attack and concentrate on attacking them. The Old Yang Style of Taiji is not a self defence system it is a defeat the opponent system.

The system could be altered so that it becomes non lethal so that it could be used by the police and security staff. The problem is that altering it makes it less effective.

Question.

So would you win a full contact competition ?

Answer.

First of all I would never enter a competition nor would I recommend any of my students to because I don't train or teach anything that is relevant for competitions. The emphasis in The Old Yang Style is to kill the opponent, we first disable them by striking their eyes to blind them and then we punch and elbow them in the throat and neck repeatedly with fa jin and dim mak. The main target areas eyes, neck and throat that we are trained to attack are always forbidden target areas in competitions so we would not be able to use our taiji.

In the Old Yang Style there is no such thing as scoring points or getting the opponent to tap out, all we do is go for the kill. When the system is applied this way it is very effective but as soon as you alter the style to make it suitable for a competition its effectiveness is significantly reduced.

If there was a compertition in which strikes to the eyes, neck and throat were allowed then people would be permanently blinded and others would die. Any one who would want to enter a compertition in which they knew that they would possibly blind or kill an opponent is not someone who I would teach.

In taiji there are only two areas, training with our training partners, or the real life fight to the death situation where there is no mercy and no runner up prize. We do not have anything in between, there are no taiji competitions nor do we incourage our students to fight with other martial arts schools. It is very enjoyable to discuss with practitioners of other styles the similarities and diffrences of our martial arts but this is in the spirit of friendship not aggressive compertition. We demonstrate moves, methods and principles but this is diffrent from a fight.

We cannot have tests of fighting skill with other martial artists because all the moves in taiji are so extreme and the strategy that we apply them with is cold hearted and ruthless. As soon as a person becomes an opponent we launch an unrelenting preemptive attack with punches to the throat, spear fingers to the eyes and repetitive elbow strikes to their neck and throat. In a fight winning is the purpose not the taking part.

In our training with our taiji training partners who we are trying to help to develop their abilities there is great emphasis on skill and it is an art. If challenged by another martial artist or by a thug on the street there is no skill, there is no art we are just brutal and ruthless in the extreme, we have to be to survive. The fighting side of taiji is interesting and the training helps to improve our health. I am an however an Acupuncturist and practitioner of Chinese Herbal Medicine, I spend my days healing people of illness and injury, so to enter a competition to intentionally cause possibly fatal internal injury and permanent mutilation to someone else for a trophy or prize money goes against my medical training.

Question.
Would you win a competition in which people were awarded points for performing their forms ?

Answer.
The Old Yang Style of Taiji is an Internal Martial Art, the forms contain internal energy work (the qi gong explained in the Internal Power chapter) that cannot be seen and the use of mental intention that cannot be seen. So how can points be awarded ?

Also when done correctly all the Old Yang Style forms have every move as a fa jin, it is nothing like the slow flowing taiji that every one else practices. Some other styles do there forms fast but that is not the same as fa jin.

When we do the Old Yang forms its like an angry snake striking or a shark in a feeding frenzy and looks nothing like what people imagine taiji should be like. The judges, if they were from other styles would say it was not taiji and if they were from the Old Yang style, they would not be judges at a competition.

Question.
Would you win a pushing hands competition ?

Answer.
The pushing hands of The Old Yang Style of Taiji is different from the other styles, they push, we strike with fa jin. In fact the Old Yang Pushing Hands should really be called Striking Hands. So it just could not be used in a competition, the other competitors would be trying to push and pull each other over or lock and throw each other or wrestle.

In the Old Yang style as soon as you make contact you hit them. For example, Tiger Paw Punch them in the side of the throat and then follow up with an Elbow Strike to the neck and Tiger Claws to the eyes pulling their head back hitting them with a Penetration Punch to the other side of the throat and then hit their decending head with your rising knee to finishing them off.

So when we practice our pushing hands it has nothing to do with competitions, it is a training method in which we work very carfully with a partner to develop fa jin and dim mak.

Question.
All the other taiji teachers I have seen show how taiji can be used to push the opponent away or pull him over or put him in a lock or throw him to the ground, surely this is enough for self defence. Why do you teach the really extreme fa jin dim mak strikes as the applications of taiji.

Answer.

If a girl is being kidnapped by a phycopathic serial killer rapist and no one is going to rescue her and she has to fight for her life. Do you really think that pushing or pulling or locking and throwing is going to be of any use what so ever or that these types of moves are going to be able to be used when she is being attacked with continuos full power punches to the face ?

For her to survive and not become a rape and murder victim she has to fight for her life, there is no other way to do this than try and kill the opponent with fa jin and dim mak, any thing less and he will achieve his objective. So it would be wrong for me to teach my students things which wouldn't work when they needed something real.

Question.

But what if it was not an extream situation would you still hit the opponent ?

Answer.

How do you know in advance wether it is going to be an extream situation or not ? What do you mean by not extream ? Are you suggesting that you wouldn't mind bieng beaten up as long as you are not going to be killed, maybe the attacker only ment to beat you up and not kill you but you die because he accidentaly hits you in the throat not the face.

It is clear to me that if I am attacked I should defend myself and not let myself get hit, I consider bieng physicaly attacked an extream situation and would hit the opponent. You cannot duck and weave to avoid their punches indefinatly, eventualy you will be hit and then hit again. And if he is close enough to hit or stab you then turning to run away is madness, he will just hit or stab you in the back of the head.

If you push or pull or throw the opponent they will just get more angry and reattack with even more aggression. And if you put them into a lock or hold they will go bezerk and thrash out trying to strike you with their free hand, head, feet etc. If a person is fired up it is impossible to put a lock on them. Locks and controlling holds should only be used after the opponent has been hit hard to drain their energy and their will to fight.

If there was a situation which could be seen clearly as not an extream situation then we do have several fa jin - dim mak knock out strikes which we would use, they are all very quick and effective and only need a very small amount of power in the strike for it to work and cause full knockout but not death.

If the situation is even less extream then these strikes can also be used in a speacial way to cause what is known in western boxing terms as a technical knock out, this means that the person is still standing but totaly stunned and unable to control their body effectivly. This way the opponent is unable to attack you and you have not had to cause him any major harm.

Question.

Can you prove that Zhang san feng created The Twelve Qi Disruption Forms or that he even existed ? and can you prove that Yang Lu Chan created taiji from them?

Answer.

I can't prove these things and no one else can disprove them. It is not possible to reach back that far in time and be one hundred percent certain. However from the documentary information now available to the general public I think it very possible that he did exist and was the originator of The Twelve Qi Disruption Forms.

The whole argument about Zhang san feng is in my opinion not so important. Did Zhang san feng exist and did he created The Twelve Qi Disruption Forms or was it several generations of the inhabitance of the Liang village in the Wu dang mountain range who created the The Twelve Qi Disruption Forms ?

Did Yang Lu Chan create the whole of The Old Yang Style Taiji system himself based on the Wu dang system or did he just create the Long Form and Pushing Hands and the rest was created by his sons and grandsons?

These questions can never have definitive answers so it is best to concentrate instead on ones training. The Wu dang System and Old Yang Style are both outstanding whoever it was that created them.

Question.

Is Qi Disruption the same as hitting some one from a distance with out touching them?

Answer.

No these are different things, Qi disruption is something we do to the opponent whilst we are already physically hitting them or just before we physically hit them. The Qi disruption works on people from a very close range to unbalance and drain their energy so that they are easier to defeat with fa jin and dim mak but by itself Qi disruption is not enough to defeat them.

Something completely different to Qi disruption is the belief that you can hit someone from a distance without touching them, this is an idea that people would like to belive is true but unfortunatly it is just a dream and not a reality. The truth is that a fight involves blood and bones with bruses and breaks, the idea that you can fight without touching is a fantasy.

The people who demonstrate hitting somone without touching them always use one of their own students or a member of the public who is first hypnotised into beliving that it will work and then subconsioiusely plays along with the show. There has never been a demonstration of the ability to hit without touching used on a person who is realy filled with the fury of combat who has the intent to realy smash and crush the person demonstrating their skill of hitting without touching.

It is important to remember that the martial arts are often misrepresented to the public in books, films and theatrical performances. So unfortunatly many people belive that certain fantastic abilities are possible when in reality they are not. Or people say that genuine feats of great strength or endurance are due to mystical powers or speacial incantations when in reality they are the result of many years of hard and dedicated training and a deep understanding of body mechanics.

Question.
Do I have to study acupuncture to be able to practice dim mak?

Answer.
No you do not have to but it does help explain what you are doing. Also it is an excellent healing system which can be used to cure a very wide range of injuries and illnesses. We should also remember that Zhang san fen (Chang san feng) was an acupuncturist and so was Chang yui chun.

Question.
Does dim mak really work ?

Answer.
Yes it really works because if you hit a person with the extreme force of fa jin on the acupuncture points that are on the most weak and vulnerable areas of the body you are going to get a big effect.

The acupuncture points that we use for dim mak are over major nerves and blood vessels and the most vulnerable parts of the neck and skull. Many of them are also right over major internal organs. Even if you do not hit the point exactly but are in roughly the right area it will still work.

Question.
Will you teach me Dim Mak?

Answer.
I could list for you which are the acupuncture points that we use for Dim mak but this is not enough. You need to have a system that teaches you how to hit these points in the right way with fa jin whilst fighting. The Old Yang Style Taiji System and The Twelve Qi disruption Forms and Twelve Hand Weapons are some of the best methods for teaching these things.

Question.
Can you teach me to strike as powerfully and as fast as I possibly can and to move with subconscious reflex actions ?

Answer.
Fa jin contains all these things and much more. Learn fa jin and all the healing and martial benefits of taiji can be yours. If a person says that they are practising taiji but do not have fa jin then it is not taiji, remember TAIJI IS FA JIN.

Question.

What move would you use if I attacked you with a hook punch or a straight jab or a front kick etc ?

Answer.

If we were in a warm blooded training situation then there are many responses that we train to counter each of these types of attack but when we fight for real it is cold blooded and we do not know what we are going to do. This is because it is not our conscious minds that thinks about what the opponent has done and then what we should respond with, this is far to slow. Rather we let our subconscious mind have a spontaneous instant reaction with whatever is appropriate at the time with no conscious thought. If taiji is applied correctly we only consciously know what we have done after our subconscious mind has already done it.

It is not really us that defeats the opponent, by this I mean our conscious mind, our personality, the person who you are that socialises and talks with other people. What defeats the opponent is a reflex survival mechanism controlled by the reptile brain. It is a part of us that most people never access and are unaware of. Taiji for fighting is a method of reactivating this often dormant part of ourselves and getting it to work for our benefit. All the moves that we have in taiji are designed to be the ones that are easiest for this part of us to express itself through.

The way taiji works is that people who all to easily slip into their reptile mode and are unable to control their rage find through the training control and understanding about who they are and how they work. So they become more civilised and mature people. And for people who are not aware of it and are to timid and weak the discovery of their reptile mind and the power, confidence and strength that it brings them enables them to walk tall in their lives and achieve there objectives.

Question.

Do you train and teach taiji as a martial art for fighting or as a type of qi gong (chi kung) for healing or as a type of moving meditation for spiritual development ? and is it better than any other system ?

Answer.

I do taiji for all these reasons they complement and balance one another very well. When I teach taiji I explain all three aspects to the students. If a student wants to concentrate on certain areas more than others then I will explain in greater detail that aspect of the art.

Some people think that dim mak is the most important thing, others that fa jing is the priority. Also there are many who don't want any martial component to their training and just want to learn the Long Form as a slow moving Qi

gong meditation. It is normal that diffrent people want diffrent things, I
don't try to turn fighters into healers or healers into fighters. I just teach
the system and see that quite naturaly people choose to eventualy develop both
aspects because they want to be balanced within themselves.

There are many martial arts which are good for fighting, there are many
excersise systems for maintaining good health and there are many meditation
methods to aid peoples development. What makes Taiji special is that it has
the martial, healing and spiritual all happening at the same time. We do not
need to learn three diffrent systems, all three aspects are within our Taiji.

Throughout my life I would like to retain the ability to defend myself, to
maintain my health and to have a spiritual component to my life. So I train
taiji for all three reasons, to me they are all as equaly as important as each
other.

Question.
Does Taiji have a belt and grading system ?

Answer.
Different schools have there own ideas and there is no universally agreed belt
and grading system. Personally I prefer not to have belts and gradings but
just to have five levels, beginners, intermediates and advanced students,
instructors and masters.

A beginner would be a person who has learnt
The Old Yang Style Long Form
The Large San Sau Two Person Fighting Form
The Small San Sau Two Person Fighting Form
The Pauchui Cannon Fist Form
The basic Single and Double Pushing Hands and applications

An intermediate level student would be one who knew all the above plus
Da Lu stepping/striking method
The 12 Mother applications of the Small San Sau
Lung Har Chuan Dragon Prawn Boxing
The Twelve Circular Tai Chi Dim Mak Palms
Advanced Single Pushing Hands and applications with Fa jing and Dim mak
Advanced Double Pushing Hands and applications with Fa jing and Dim mak

An advanced level student would be one who knew all the above plus
The Nine Pre emptive Attacking Methods
The Hidden applications of the Pauchui Form
The Twelve Chi Disruption forms of Wu Dang
The Twelve Hand Weapons Forms of Wu Dang
The most Advanced Double Pushing Hands applications
The Taiji Weapons Forms

An instructor should know all the above and understand all of the above. Also an instructor should have got to the level where the system had started to teach them its deeper aspects. Plus of course an instructor should be able to teach all of the above in a clear effective way and be a relatively balanced easily approachable person.

To be a master means you have really mastered the whole system both the fighting and healing. This is only possible if you have been practising the whole system for a very very long time.

This idea I have about five levels is not a fixed unchangeable structure, it is just a rough outline so that people can see how far they are on their own path of development. Also the order is not fixed and unchangeable, a beginner might do a few intermediate and advanced things as well. People should not get to fixated on belts or levels, just train every day and gradualy make progress.

Question.
If you have any more questions please email me   paul@taiji.net
or call me on 020 8264 8074
or write to me at PO BOX 13219, LONDON NW11 7WS, ENGLAND UK

About the author

Paul Brecher BA FAcS began training in the martial arts at the age of ten and is now the Senior Instructor for the World Taiji Boxing Association in London. He is also a lecturer at The College of Chinese Medicine in London where he teaches Acupuncture and Chinese Herbal Medicine.

He has made numerous appearances on television, been interviewed on radio and in the national press. And his books 'The Principles of Tai Chi' and 'The Way Of The Spiritual Warrior' and 'Tai Chi Directions' and 'The Secrets of Energy Work' are all sold worldwide.

Paul Brecher BA FAcS has his own medical practice in London where he treats patients with Acupuncture and Chinese Herbal Medicine to make an appointment please call 020 8264 8074

If you would like to study Taiji or Acupuncture and Chinese Herbal Medicine then please visit

www.taiji.net

Paul can also be contacted at

PAUL BRECHER
PO BOX 13219
LONDON NW11 7WS
ENGLAND UK

paul@taiji.net

Telephone 020 8 264 8074